Irises
Jennifer He...

bulleyane

All drawings, including the front cover, by Gillian Ingram
Edited and typeset by George Parker
Consultant editor to the Booklet Series: Tony Lord

© The Hardy Plant Society – April 2003
ISBN 0 901687 20 0

Iris bucharica

Acknowledgements

My thanks are due first, and very sincerely, to Gillian Ingram for the illustrations. Not being as familiar with irises as she would have liked, she was initially doubtful about the job but allowed herself to be persuaded. Having admired her work in other HPS booklets I was delighted and confident that the results would enhance the text and am sure readers will agree. If it was a steep learning curve she has conquered it. We would both like to thank Olga Wells for all her help in providing irises that we wished to have illustrated but were not growing at Copton Ash, and Tim Ingram for his help also.

No one person can know everything about such a large and varied genus and, without years of friendship, information and help from British Iris Society members, especially Sidney Linnegar but others too numerous to mention, on which I have drawn heavily, this booklet could not have been written. I am grateful to you all. And to George Parker for helpful editing and Tony Lord for checking facts and filling in gaps in my knowledge and memory. It only remains to say that any errors are those I have achieved all by myself.

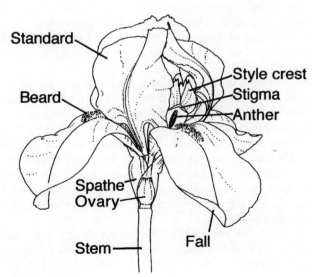

Parts of the iris flower

Introduction

IN MANY PARTS OF THE WORLD it would be possible to have a garden growing nothing but irises and have something of interest throughout the year - flowers, foliage and seeds. That would be carrying devotion to the genus to extremes, not least because irises combine well with, and enhance, other plants as well as being included on their own merits. In addition to their year-round potential they have flowers of architectural form in almost the widest possible range of colours and many sizes, on stems from one centimetre to over two metres tall carrying anything from a single flower to twenty or more. Leaves can be upright or arching, sometimes variegated; some turn gold and bronze in autumn, others are evergreen and especially valuable in winter when seed heads too come into their own. Those of *Iris foetidissima* are well known, as the seeds, in vermilion, yellow or white, stay attached to the pods until spring, but there are other irises whose pods, without seeds, contribute to the winter garden. And there can be few places where the winter-flowering irises are not grown and welcomed as harbingers of spring and summer and the glorious main season of bloom.

Do they flower for too short a time to be worth garden space? It is true that there are a few species whose flowers last for less than a day but with the great majority a single bloom normally lasts four to five days, which is equal to many perennials. With blooms opening in succession on each stem a clump with a number of stems will give a display for a month or longer, even for several months. And few other genera can provide the glamour that iris flowers possess.

No one species or group of cultivars is going to combine all these qualities but most have several to recommend them. Then there is the wide variety of habitats in which they are found in the wild, which means there are irises for most garden conditions and situations in temperate climates. There are those that grow almost as far north as the Arctic Circle and, at the other extreme, species from habitats that are almost subtropical or endure hot dry summers in near-desert conditions. Yet others grow in water or soils that are moist for most of the time. Some are undoubtedly difficult to grow away from their natural environment, even in very suitable sites, but most fit into gardens in temperate climatic zones very readily.

This booklet cannot cover the entire range but more detailed information can be found in others. And when buying, do try to see irises in flower or photographs, as both are more helpful than brief descriptions.

Geography and Botany

THE GENUS *IRIS* IS A VERY LARGE ONE, containing over 200 species plus subspecies, forms, variants and natural hybrids and thousands of cultivars that have arisen in gardens, either by chance pollination by insects or by design, since deliberate hybridization has been widely practised since the late 19th century.

Irises belong to the family *Iridaceae*, a family that includes many other iridaceous genera. Whilst irises are native to only the northern hemisphere, south of the equator there are irids such as *Schizostylis, Watsonia* and *Moraea,* and other more widespread relatives include *Crocus, Sisyrinchium* and *Gladiolus.*

Europe, Asia, North Africa and North America provide homes for different iris species though some can be found in more than one continent. Two species are native to the British Isles, many more spread throughout mainland Europe and its islands and into Russia, whilst bulbs and some of the most exotic looking inhabit dry and semi-desert areas in the Middle East and North Africa. Then they reach right across central Asia to the Himalaya and beyond; China is rich in species including two from almost subtropical regions, and Japan shares this rich flora. Furthest north in Europe and Asia is *Iris setosa,* which comes close to circling the globe by turning up in Alaska and across North America where there are other irises found only in the USA and Canada, reaching the far south and, again, almost subtropical conditions.

With such a wide distribution and with irises having evolved in different climates and soils, some are closely related, others more distantly. So the genus is divided into subgenera, sections and series according to these relationships, though all share some characteristics. These divisions will be followed in this booklet and will reflect current classification but DNA analyses already being carried out indicate that there will be considerable revision in the future.

Botanical features that characterise the *Iridaceae* distinguish them from other plant families and the most obvious is that all parts of the flower are based on the number three. This may not always be obvious at first sight; some irids have parts in multiples of three but look closely at an iris and it will be seen that there are three inner petals, three outer ones which are, botanically, sepals and that the style which carries the stigmas divides into three at some point.

The diagram of an iris flower (page 3) shows the names given to these

5

parts. The inner three (true) petals are the standards which may be held vertically or nearly so but can flare outwards, be horizontal, or droop to lie over and between the falls, whilst in Juno irises they are usually downturned. In bearded irises the standards can be big and showy, sometimes bigger than the falls, but among the beardless they vary considerably in size and position and sometimes are almost invisible, being just tiny bristles. The sepals, often called petals for convenience, form the falls, which do generally conform to their name. An easy way to remember which is which is that the standards stand up and the falls fall down, even if neither statement is entirely true. Falls can vary from being horizontal, often arching downwards towards the tips, or hang more or less vertically. They are usually, but not always, larger than the standards or may appear smaller because the tips are deeply reflexed back towards the stem. The inner, narrower parts of both standards and falls are called the hafts, and in bearded irises this is where the beard, a line of short bushy hairs, begins. It extends onto the upper part of the blade (the wider part) of the falls. Some species have beards on the standards too.

One of the major divisions, botanically and for gardeners too, is between bearded and beardless irises, and not just because some have this feature and others do not. The beardless irises are a more diverse group with a wider range of habitats in the wild and in gardens. The function of the beard is not clear; it does not seem to be a guide for insects but most beardless irises have, in the same area, a patch called the signal, which does guide insects to the nectar at the base of the falls. Some irises in the beardless group and some bulbous ones have noticeable ridges or crests in place of beards, and signals too.

The third major feature of iris flowers is the style arms, springing from the centre of the flower to arch over the hafts of the falls. Whereas in other flowers, including some irids, the style is slender and divides into three near its upper end, in irises it divides not far above the base of the flower into wide, 'petaloid' arms that end in upward-curling crests. The colouring of these arms is often very beautiful and subtle, adding greatly to the appearance of the flower.

Just below the crest is the stigma itself. In bearded irises it is a narrow lip, shown on the diagram, but beardless irises usually have a small triangular stigma that is less obvious. But in any type of iris it may be coloured differently from the style arm, which is a help if deliberate hybridising is being done. When the flower first unfurls, the stigma is pressed tightly against the style arm but as it develops it bends forwards and what is then its upper surface becomes slightly sticky so that pollen grains can adhere and grow down to the ovary. The anthers that carry pollen are found between the hafts of the falls and style arms. Two sacs are also tightly closed to start with but later they open and release white, cream or pale blue pollen grains that are easily visible.

In bud, the flower is enclosed by spathes but it grows out of them before opening and the spathes, which may stay green or go papery brown, remain below, covering the ovary. This is little more than a bulge on the stem but when the ovules in its three chambers are fertilised and develop into seeds, the ovary swells. Most seedpods are noticeable but larger ones on bigger plants are especially prominent. Some irises, such as *Iris unguicularis,* have only a tiny true stem with a long perianth tube opening into the flower at the top, and consequently their seedpods are at or close to ground level and easily missed. This can lead to seedlings growing in the parent clump and being confused with it, which may not matter much in the case of pure species that have not been cross-pollinated by relatives growing close by, but can lead to a lot of confusion. So cut off pods as soon as they are ripe or, if the seeds are not wanted, remove the pods as soon as the flowers fade. In about twelve weeks the seeds should be ripe and the pods begin to turn brown and split at the top. Most seeds are more or less D-shaped and some shade of brown or of a greenish colour; those of *I. foetidissima* are red, yellow or white and, unlike others, they stay attached to the pods until spring. Seeds of water irises are buoyant so that they float to a new home, Louisiana irises particularly so, as they have a thick corky coat.

Stems can be from slender to stout, anything from one centimetre to over two metres tall, with one or two flowers or branches carrying from three to twenty or more.

At the base of the flower stem is a fan of leaves growing from the rhizome or bulb. Leaves vary in length and in breadth, from fine and grassy to quite broad, held vertically or arching over. As well as various shades of green they can be glaucous (bluish), or yellow-toned, and variegated foliage has lengthwise stripes of yellow, cream or white.

Irises store food in order to produce leaves and flowers but do this in different ways. Many have rhizomes, which are usually horizontal, growing at or just below the soil surface. Brown, yellow or green, the woody rhizomes are covered with the scars of old leaf bases. They develop from seeds or from little buds at the sides of previous rhizomes and grow longer and larger until they reach flowering size, always with the fan of leaves at the outer end. Some irises need only small rhizomes while those that produce the taller, stouter stems will have the largest ones. Some species of Section *Lophiris*, the Evansias, have vertical green rhizomes known as canes, up to two metres tall. After a rhizome of whatever size has bloomed, it dies but offsets will be developing for future blooms.

The other main type of storage organ is a bulb. Well-known bulbous irises include the Reticulatas and the larger Dutch, Spanish and 'English' irises. The largest group is that of the Junos and they have additional storage in the form of fleshy tuberous roots below the bulb. These are as essential as the bulb itself and must be carefully handled to avoid damage; if they are lost or badly damaged the whole plant may well die. Many Junos are rare and need specialised cultivation, if they can be obtained at all.

Some irises, both bearded and beardless, produce a rhizome or bulb at the end of an over- or underground stolon and in Subgenus *Nepalensis* there is a minute rhizome or growing point with tuberous roots.

All the storage organs are fed by a network of fine roots. When these grow close to the soil surface, as they do in most rhizomatous irises, they are easily damaged by hoeing or careless cultivation.

Iris reticulata

Cultivation and Hardiness

A S THERE IS SUCH VARIETY among irises and the conditions they need, each group will have its needs given individually. What can be generally said is that, though many will grow in shade, they need warmth to ripen their rhizomes or bulbs and develop flower buds, so sun for at least part of the day is usually necessary. In regions with very hot dry summers, irises go dormant in summer, starting into growth again with autumn rains and then flowering and setting seed swiftly in spring. Gardeners in such areas can grow irises that are difficult in cooler, damper climates but may find that without some shade the plants can be killed by heat. Deeper planting than is generally recommended is another necessity.

Cold-hardiness, too, is a very variable character. The most widely grown, deciduous groups are normally hardy in Zone 7 and possibly Zone 6 if given protection such as a covering of conifer boughs, but another factor may be the amount of winter wet. Snow, if thick and long lasting, is a form of protection but light falls that melt quickly and then maybe freeze, or a generally wet winter with sharp frosts at times, can be fatal. Evergreen irises may not be completely killed where winters are long and cold but damage to their leaves is debilitating and can eventually lead to death.

A few species, *Iris speculatrix* and *I. formosana* from southern China and some - not all - of the Louisiana irises native to the southern USA, can tolerate little if any frost. Cultivars of hardier types that have been bred in warmer climates may perform less well in colder areas. The allocation to a climate zone can offer a guide, but a broad one, as the degree of hardiness of any plant can be affected by situation within a zone and within a garden, and by other factors such as soil and precipitation. There is general advice given for each group but eventually it comes down to the gardener knowing the area and the garden, and learning from experience.

Propagation and Hybridizing

DIVISION

The only way to propagate named cultivars is by division. As most of them are hybrids they will not come true from seed. Even if a seedling looks similar to its parent it should not be called by the parent's name as it will almost certainly be genetically different and may very well be inferior.

Growth buds develop at the sides of rhizomes, usually close to the main fan first, and take a year or more to grow to flowering size in their turn. It is better not to divide small plants but wait until they increase and can make several divisions, and while a single large rhizome, for example that of a tall bearded, can establish itself, the smaller bearded and most beardless irises should have at least two to four rhizomes in a clump. Some irises can resent being moved, *Iris unguicularis* being one of them, and leaving half the clump *in situ* and moving only the other half is a way of insuring against losing the whole plant. Even when a plant is obviously not happy it may be better not to disturb all of it unless it is very small, until you are sure the new situation is a better one.

Irises make most of their new root growth soon after flowering finishes and this is generally the best time for dividing and transplanting, but it can be done carefully at any time between spring and autumn providing the weather will encourage them to settle in and continue growing, i.e. it is not too hot. Pacific Coast Irises, in most places, are definitely better transplanted in cooler conditions, usually early autumn. All dead material, such as spent rhizomes, and weak pieces should be discarded. Cut large rhizomes off cleanly where they join others and divide clumps of small rhizomes such as those of Siberians by using two forks back to back. Do not allow the roots to dry out, in particular those of beardless irises and PCIs; cover them, heel them in or keep them in water until they can be replanted.

Bulbous irises produce bulblets at the bases of their bulbs that can be left to grow on *in situ* or be removed to a nursery bed. A clump that is not flowering and has poor leaves is probably overcrowded. Lift the whole clump and divide it and replant healthy bulbs at the original depth after adding fertiliser to the site.

RAISING IRISES FROM SEED

It is as easy to raise irises from seed as any other plants - easier than some, as the seeds are a comfortable size to handle. They can be sown in spring or in autumn as soon as they are ripe; spuria seeds are said to germinate best if sown while they are still green. All of them germinate better if they are soaked in tap water, changed daily, for four to seven days; seeds of water irises will float but others should sink when they have absorbed sufficient water. They can then be mixed with moist peat or vermiculite in a closed bag or container and kept in the refrigerator (not the freezer) for three weeks. Or they may be exposed to cold weather outside, but protect them from birds, cats or other disturbance.

It is safer to sow seeds in pots than in the open ground, spacing them out so the seedlings will not be too crowded. Use a good seed compost with extra grit added when good drainage is essential, sow the seeds on top and cover lightly with compost or grit. Use a lime-free medium for irises that dislike lime. Seeds of water irises need to be kept wet, others just moist. When the seedlings have three to four leaves or are about 15cm (6in) high they can be pricked out, but if they reach this size late in the season they may be safer in individual pots in a cold frame for the winter. They should be planted 15-30cm (6-12in) apart, depending on the size they will attain when mature, with the crown just below the soil surface.

HYBRIDIZING

This is a fascinating way of raising your own new cultivars; gardening is a creative activity, and hybridizing even more so. Using related parents, making crosses between for example two Tall Beardeds or two Siberians, is most likely to be successful and lead to further generations. Crossing irises from different groups can be more difficult and the resulting seedlings may well be sterile.

The drawing showing the parts of an iris indicates the parts you will need. On a dry day, remove the anthers and falls from the irises that are to be the parents as the flowers begin to open, before insects can get at them. The anthers should be closed but a few hours in a dry, not too hot, place should see them open to release the pollen grains. By then the stigmas on the chosen pod (female) parent should have bent forward, showing they are receptive. Hold an anther in tweezers, gently brush it across the upper surface of the stigma (the one that was pressed against the underside of the style arm) and the deposited pollen should be visible. Repeat with the other stigmas and anthers on the same flower.

Record the cross, writing (pod parent's name) x (pollen parent's name) on a label and tying it to the stem, and record it in a notebook too - labels can fade. The ovary should soon start to swell and about three months later begin to split at the top. Harvest the seeds and sow them as above. There may be flowers a year after the cross was made but two or three years is more likely. If you think you have something worth trialling by other people, arrange for this, or get in touch with the RHS or the British Iris Society.

Pests and Diseases

HOLES CHEWED IN RHIZOMES AND LEAVES are not only unsightly, they admit diseases, so deal with slugs and snails by whatever methods you prefer. Dead leaves on bearded or evergreen irises should be gently pulled away from the rhizomes and deciduous beardless irises should be trimmed back to 15cm (6in) or so in autumn. The remains will come away easily during the spring clean up.

Viruses are spread by aphids, which should be controlled by removing them physically or by the use of appropriate pesticides. With changes being made (at the time of writing) to chemicals that are approved for use in gardens in the UK and that are available to amateur gardeners, it is difficult to make specific recommendations. Consult the Pesticides Safety Directory website, www.secure.pesticides.gov.uk or see what products are on sale in shops and garden centres, reading the labels carefully. There may be equivalent websites in other countries where the range of available products may be different from that in Britain.

Vine weevils present an increasing problem and have been reported as killing *Iris ensata* (Japanese iris) cultivars in Devon, England, in pots and the open ground. Again, if this trouble is experienced it will be necessary to check on what measures can be taken to deal with it. There may be products, including biological control, which can be used, but make sure that you are using the right one, depending on whether it is for containers and the open ground, or for one but not the other.

Diseases can affect plants before any symptoms are seen, which makes them hard to control. One of the commonest is bacterial soft rot, which is likely to affect bearded irises growing in poorly drained soil or a damp climate or in a long spell of wet weather. Slug damage to rhizomes allows the bacteria to enter and the first sign is often yellow leaf tips, followed by the whole fan falling over or coming away if it is grasped. Another source of trouble can be the remains of flowering stems that have not been cut right back to the rhizomes. At the base of the fan, spreading from the rhizome, is a foul-smelling yellowish mush. Cut back the rhizome to clean white tissue, scrape the soil away from all cut surfaces, dust them with green or yellow sulphur and watch to make sure the problem does not recur. All the infected material should be disposed of; burn it if possible and never put it on the compost heap. Sterilize your knife and wash your hands thoroughly, and do this between plants if there is more than one to be treated.

Leaf spot is a fungal disease that can appear on the leaves of bearded irises in warm moist weather. Small black blotches get rapidly larger until the leaf withers away. Spray with myclobutanil or penconazole to control the problem. The same treatment should be used for botrytis (grey mould), which may attack some beardless irises, and rust, which is usually less serious, on both beardeds and beardless. With botrytis the same weather conditions can result in leaves going first yellow, then brown, and collapsing, and grey mould becoming visible at the base of the leaf fans. Siberian irises seem rather prone to botrytis, especially in mass plantings on heavy ground, but it rarely happens in mixed plantings. A preventive spray, before any signs are seen, can be applied if the problem has occurred previously.

Ink Disease can attack Reticulatas and other bulbous irises, premature yellowing of the leaves being the first symptom to be seen. There is no cure at present. Dig up the bulbs and if they have black spots or streaks, burn or otherwise dispose of them and the leaves and do not plant new bulbs in those places unless the soil has been sterilised.

Aphids and the use of infected tools can spread Iris Mosaic and other viruses, which seem to have little or no effect as a rule. However, if flowers and foliage are badly marked or deformed, the plants should be dug up and disposed of, as there is no cure. Take care when buying plants and try to avoid infected ones.

Irises in Company

MANY IRISES COMBINE WELL with other plants, especially perennials and alpines, though companions will of course be chosen according to the conditions they and the irises require. This section will contain some suggestions for combinations but there are many more possibilities. Whilst the gardener's personal preferences must be his guide, it is important to think of where irises will grow best and there are other factors to be considered.

Spiky foliage makes a good contrast with the rounded shape of other plant clumps: a good reason for including irises in beds, borders, bogs or ponds, not least because even deciduous leaves last for longer than most flowers. But there are also other things to think of - soil, for example. Is it acid, neutral, alkaline? There are irises that prefer each kind and some do poorly in the wrong type while others are tolerant of any soil that is not very acid or alkaline; many grow happily in a pH of 6.5 - 7.5. Is the soil a heavy clay or very sandy? Either will limit the choice or need ameliorating. Most bearded and bulbous irises require good drainage but sandy soil can be very low in nutrients, whilst the beardless are more variable but, with a few exceptions, require soils that hold some moisture or even need to grow in permanent water. Sunny and shady sites are both possible but the degree of shade can affect the ability of an iris to flower, even to grow well. And thuggish companions are not generally welcome though just a few irises are strong enough to hold their own.

Something that must be watched in the case of bearded irises is that their rhizomes are not overgrown by leafy, spreading plants, for example alpine campanulas on the rock garden or hardy geraniums in the border. Not only because the rhizomes need sun; they can rot if covered by other plants that keep them damp or provide lurking places for slugs and snails that chew rhizomes and leaves, and then disease has easy access. Interplanting with bulbous irises or other bulbs without too much foliage such as tulips, camassias, hardy gladioli and other hardy irids, or adding less hardy ones for the summer - large-flowered gladioli or watsonias, for example - gives a succession of colour. Hemerocallis, non-aggressive geraniums, dieramas, taller campanulas, are all possible companions. Perennials forming compact but dense clumps, such as Michaelmas daisies or aconitums, are better used as a background because of the shade they can cast, and the same is true of tall artemisias though irises teamed with silver or glaucous foliage are very effective. Pinks, *Dianthus* species and cultivars, and other low-growing 'silvers' make good edgings as long as they do not spread over the irises. Most beardless irises are very good mixers. Siberians and the spurias do well in borders, the taller ones adding height to a planting and those of middling size or shorter for more forward positions, and there are few perennials whose company they do not enjoy. When well established they can tolerate drought, if not too prolonged, but a fairly open but moisture-retentive soil suits them best. Perennials for similar conditions include pulmonarias in the foreground for early spring flowers and their foliage as well as that of hostas through the summer, especially if the pulmonarias get some shade from taller plants in all but cool gardens. Aquilegias and thalictrums provide contrasts in form and texture as do actaeas (formerly called cimicifugas) later in summer, and the brilliant colours of *Schizostylis coccinea* complement the irises' autumn colouring.

Providing the soil is neutral to acid Pacific Coast, or Californian, irises look good with the same companions, or make good ground cover amongst ericaceous shrubs as the irises usually appreciate some shade in southern Britain and similar climates.

The Japanese irises, cultivars developed from the species *Iris ensata,* form another popular group for acid soil. Though they need moist soil they are not water irises. Astilbes, hostas and thalictrums are just a few of the perennials to grow with them. *Iris setosa* is another species for similar conditions, whilst the British native *I. foetidissima* will grow almost anywhere, even in dry shade, but is happier and more rewarding given better treatment.

In or close to water there are species and cultivars that are invaluable and look well with most moisture-loving plants: primulas, ferns, sedges (*Carex* species), astilbes - the choice is limited only by space and the gardener's preferences.

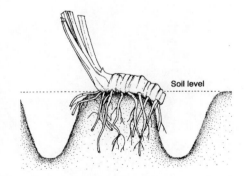

Soil level

Planting an iris to expose the rhizome to the sun

Awards

NOT ALL GOOD IRISES, whether hardy or not, get awards but it can be helpful to know which have succeeded in garden trials. These normally last for three years at least, so that the plants can become established before being judged on their health and ability to increase satisfactorily as well as their flower and foliage qualities. The Royal Horticultural Society (RHS) runs such trials in Britain leading to the Award of Garden Merit (AGM) and irises from any country may be included. National iris societies in several countries have their own garden trials and awards, the top one being the Dykes Medal (DM), which is awarded annually to the best iris of whatever type. The British Iris Society (BIS) trials include irises bred in other European countries; the American Iris Society (AIS) judges those from Canada as well as the USA; and the iris societies of Australia and New Zealand also award Dykes Medals to irises bred in their respective countries. Each country, and others, has other awards too, usually given to specific groups.

An iris that wins an award will not necessarily do well in every situation though the specialist societies' judging is based on performance in several locations. So although the awards are mentioned in the lists of recommendations, it is still essential to choose the right plant for the place where you want to grow it.

THE IRIS CALENDAR: Months of the year in which Irises give value

FLOWERS OR FRUITS:	J	F	M	A	M	J	J	A	S	O	N	D
IN THE GARDEN												
Iris unguicularis & cultivars	◆	◆	◆							◆	◆	◆
I. histrioides, I. danfordiae	◆	◆										
I. reticulata and cultivars		◆	◆									
Juno irises (hardy)			◆	◆								
Dwarf Bearded species & cultivars				◆	◆							
Intermediate Bearded cultivars					◆							
Bearded species (except dwarf)					◆	◆						
Tall Bearded cultivars					◆	◆						
Bulbous Spanish & Dutch irises				◆	◆	◆						
Pacific Coast species & cultivars					◆	◆						
Evansia irises (hardy)					◆	◆						
I. setosa & forms						◆						
Siberian irises						◆						
Chrysographes species & cultivars						◆	◆					
I. laevigata & cultivars						◆	◆					
I. pseudacorus, I. versicolor						◆	◆					
I. foetidissima & forms						◆	◆					
I. foetidissima seedpods	◆	◆								◆	◆	◆
Spuria irises						◆	◆					
Louisiana irises						◆	◆					
Other beardless irises						◆	◆					
I. ensata & cultivars						◆	◆	◆				
Bulbous English irises						◆	◆					
Remontant Siberian cultivars					◆	◆	◆	◆	◆			
Remontant bearded cultivars					◆	◆		◆	◆	◆		
UNDER GLASS												
Evansia & Juno irises	◆	◆	◆	◆	◆							
Aril irises				◆	◆	◆						
Bulbous irises	◆	◆			◆							
VARIEGATED FOLIAGE												
I. pallida, I. ensata			◆	◆	◆	◆	◆	◆	◆			
I. foetidissima, I. japonica	◆	◆	◆	◆	◆	◆	◆	◆	◆	◆	◆	◆
I. pseudacorus			◆	◆	◆							

Bearded Irises

THESE ARE GROUPED INTO SIX SECTIONS and the largest and most important to gardeners is Section *Iris*, also known as the Pogons, often and wrongly listed as *Iris germanica*. As well as a range of species there is a huge, sometimes bewildering, number of cultivars. No one wants to plant a dwarf iris behind taller plants or plan a grouping to flower together only to find the iris is out of step, so the AIS, which is the International Cultivar Registration Authority for rhizomatous irises, has classified them according to their height and flowering season and these groups are described on pages 18-28. As a rough guide, it will be seen that the shortest are the earliest to flower, after which they get taller and later.

The other five sections of Subgenus *Iris*, *Psammiris*, *Oncocyclus*, *Regelia*, *Hexapagon* and *Pseudoregelia*, whose seeds have a white or cream appendage, the aril, at one end are named for this feature. The majority of Arils come from the Middle East and parts of Asia that are very dry, almost deserts, in summer, have rain in autumn and spring and can be under snow for much of the winter so stay relatively dry. If these conditions can be met it may be possible to grow Aril irises in the garden but not all of them are cold-hardy. In Britain they are mostly best grown under glass though there are some exceptions.

CULTIVATION

In the garden, all bearded irises need plenty of sun and well-drained soil, preferably slightly alkaline; acid soil should have lime added to it. Heavy soils should have grit and humus dug in to improve drainage. The planting diagram (p.15) shows the best position, with at least half the rhizome above the soil surface, though they may be set a little deeper to begin with to allow for settlement. On sandy soils they can be planted deeper and in hotter climates than Britain's they may need to have 3-5 cm (1-2ins) covering the rhizomes to protect them from strong summer heat. Other than this, and covering with conifer branches in winter in areas of deep and prolonged cold for a different kind of protection, they should never be mulched as they are likely to rot and almost certainly will flower poorly or not at all.

When preparing to plant bearded irises by all means dig in well-rotted garden compost or manure, spent hops or mushroom compost but put it where the roots will reach it and have a layer of soil topping the mound on which the rhizomes sit. Slow-release fertiliser can be gently forked in around the planted rhizomes and a general fertiliser can be used for top-dressing in spring. Never use any feed that is high in nitrogen as this leads to soft growth susceptible to disease, or leaves at the expense of flowers. Alternatively, make up a dressing of 4 parts by weight of bonemeal, 2 parts superphosphate of lime and 1 part each of sulphate of ammonia and sulphate of potash, mixing it thoroughly and applying it at 60-75g per m^2 (2-2½ oz per yd^2).

It is sometimes suggested that the leaves should be trimmed back to 30cm (12in) or so after flowering, so that sun can reach the rhizomes to ripen them and develop next year's flower buds, but this should not really be necessary and the leaves, while green, help to feed the rhizomes. However, when new plants or recently divided ones are being set they may be liable to wind-rock and leaves should be trimmed. If they are short of roots put a short stake behind the rhizome with a soft tie around the leaves until the roots have anchored it firmly. Leaves die back in autumn and should then be pulled away gently. Also, when flowering finishes, cut the spent stem off right back to the rhizome unless it is carrying seedpods that you want. Do not leave a stub of stem as this can rot and introduce disease.

As most new root growth develops after flowering ends, planting and replanting are ideally done at this time but if irises are being grown as part of a larger planting this may not be convenient. In that case the operation can be done in early autumn but *early* should be emphasized, as otherwise the plants can be set back and take some time to recover fully.

COLOURS, PATTERNS AND FORMS

Bearded irises come in just about every possible colour except for true red and green, though breeders are getting close to developing both. From white the spectrum runs through cream, yellows, peach, orange and apricot to yellow-toned reds and brown; while from the blue side there are pink, crimson, lilac, lavender, many blues, purple, violet, to black. Flowers often combine two or more colours in varying ways. The terms shown below are a shorthand way of describing colours and patterns.

self	single colour throughout
bitone	two tones of the same colour
amoena	white standards, coloured falls
neglecta	pale blue standards, deeper falls
variegata	yellow standards, falls red, maroon or brown
bicolor	two colours, other than amoena, neglecta or variegata
blend	a mixture of colours
plicata	white to yellow ground colour, stitched, dotted or veined in a darker colour at the petal edges
luminata	a development of the plicata pattern, the darker colour being more solid, often with pale petal edges or a halo round the beard

A recent development is 'broken' colouring, with darker, lighter, or white streaks in the flowers. Some bearded iris species have variegated foliage - the cultivar name 'Variegata' refers to this, not to the variegata colour pattern in flowers - and cultivars with variegated foliage are also being developed.

Older cultivars and species generally have rather drooping falls but nowadays the majority of cultivars have 'stronger substance', i.e. thicker petals, which not only makes flowers longer-lasting and generally more weather-resistant but gives arching or flaring falls and standards that do not collapse. Petal edges are usually waved or ruffled, attractive features as long as they are not overdone and flowers find it difficult to open, and edges may be finely serrated ('laced').

Beards can add to the interest of the flower by being differently coloured and there are now 'Space Age' irises with extensions on the beards ranging from slightly elongated points at the outer ends, known as horns, to larger and more elaborate additions named spoons and flounces. Opinions vary as to the desirability of these developments; they have arisen through hybridisers bringing out the genetic potential of some cultivars by planned breeding and not through modifications made in laboratories.

MINIATURE DWARF BEARDED (MDB) IRISES

This is the category for the smallest bearded cultivars, up to 20cm (8in) tall. They begin to flower in the middle of spring, April in Britain, and most have two flowers per stem though a few have three. Given a sunny spot on the edge of a bed, in a trough, or the rock garden, they should quite quickly make a clump with a number of stems and produce a mass of colour, as long as they are in good soil. Small plants with short roots, they can exhaust the area around their clumps in two years and need replanting in soil to which garden compost or other nourishment has been added, as described previously. When replanting discard dead or weak parts but do not divide the clumps into single rhizomes; keep them in groups of three or four as these re-establish better. The best time is soon after flowering finishes, or in late summer. Keep the plants watered until they are growing away. A top-dressing at the rate of 60g per m^2 (2oz per yd^2) in spring gives them a timely boost. Slugs and snails appreciate them too, so take precautions.

The Trials Field at the RHS Gardens at Wisley is not suitable for these little irises and none has been given an AGM, though under the old awards system the deep violet-blue **'Marhaba'** gained a First Class Certificate in 1971, and it is still a good iris. The AIS awards the Caparne-Welch Medal to the best in this category, each year. Some cultivars that can be recommended are

'Alpine Lake' 18cm (7in), white standards, very pale blue falls. Caparne-

Welch Medal winner.

'Bee Wings' 15cm (6in), yellow, falls marked with maroon.

'Bright White' 18cm (7in), pure white.

'Dunlin' 15cm (6in), violet plicata on a white ground.

'Fashion Lady' 15cm (6in), yellow self.

'Garnet Elf' 18cm (7in), dark red self. Caparne-Welch Medal.

'Jasper Gem' 20cm (8in), brownish-red bitone.

'Knick-knack' 15cm (6in), white and pale purple plicata.

'Lemon Puff' 15cm (6in), lemon standards and white falls. Caparne-Welch Medal.

'Scribe' 15cm (6in), white ground veined deep violet.

MEDIAN BEARDED IRISES

This term covers four groups ranging in height from 20-70cm (8-27in) and either flowering at different times or varying in other ways. They are planted in one RHS trial at Wisley but in their separate groupings.

STANDARD DWARF BEARDED (SDB) IRISES

SDBs are generally sturdy, good-tempered plants, ideal for the front of the border; the shorter ones make good rock garden inhabitants. Flowering a little later than the MDBs, and from 20-38cm (8-15in) in height, they are normally branched with three to four flowers per stem and will make clumps 45cm (18in) or more across, covered in bloom. Planting and cultivation is the same as for the MDBs and they will probably need division and replanting every three years, a job which can be done about 6 - 8 weeks after flowering finishes. It is better to keep the rhizomes in clumps of two or three as single rhizomes are harder to establish.

There are quantities of good cultivars available, many of them old favourites such as **'Green Spot'** AGM, creamy white with olive green on the falls, which appeared in 1951. Older cultivars can have smaller flowers but have proved their staying power as garden plants while more modern varieties have better substance so the flowers last longer. The list below has been compiled to give a range of colours but could be many times longer.

'Ballet Lesson' AGM 30cm (12in), peach pink, falls with white centres.

'Bedford Lilac' AGM 28cm (11in), lilac-blue self with a deeper spot on the falls. Cook-Douglas Medal (AIS).

'Bibury' AGM 30cm (12in), white self. Dykes Medal (BIS), the only SDB to have won this top award.

'Blue Denim' 36cm (14in), medium blue self, older but reliable.

'Bromyard' AGM 30cm (12in), blue-grey standards, falls maroon and yellow.

'Eyebright' AGM 30cm (12in), bright yellow with dark brown lines on the falls.

Standard Dwarf Bearded Iris

'**Gingerbread Man**' 36cm (14in), ginger-brown self, blue beards.
'**Jeremy Brian**' AGM 25cm (10in), silvery-blue self.
'**Little Black Belt**' 30cm (12in), near-black self, pale blue beards. Cook-Douglas Medal.
'**Mary McIlroy**' AGM 30cm (12in), vivid golden/orange yellow self.

'Michael Paul' AGM 30cm (12in), dark purple self. Cook-Douglas Medal.
'Morning's Blush' AGM 36cm (14in), yellow standards, orange falls and beards.
'Pale Shades' AGM 30cm (12in), blue-white standards, buttery cream falls.
'Sun Doll' AGM 36cm (14in), medium yellow self. Cook-Douglas Medal.
'Sweet Kate' AGM 36cm (14in), bitone, lemon standards, deeper lemon falls.

INTERMEDIATE BEARDED (IB) IRISES

These are intermediate in several senses, as their main season of bloom comes between the SDBs and the tall beardeds but they overlap with both at either end and they are intermediate in height and number of flowers per stem. Most will carry at least six flowers, having two or more branches as well as terminal blooms, and heights range from 38-70cm (16-27in). Good border plants as long as they are not overgrown, they need space to expand and should be planted around 30cm (12in) apart in sunny positions. They are useful for filling in the gap that can occur between the main spring and summer seasons, and combined with tulips can make very colourful displays.

Again, there is a great variety of colours from which to choose.
'Alison Taylor' AGM 45cm (18in), brown plicata markings on a yellow ground.
'Bronzaire' AGM 51cm (20in), golden bronze self, very free-flowering.
'Cannington Skies' 45cm (18in), sky blue self with white beards, ruffled.
'Cee Jay' AGM 61cm (24in), white and violet plicata. Sass Medal (AIS).
'Clara Garland' AGM 51cm (20in), bright yellow, falls lined with brown.
'Katie-Koo' AGM 51cm (20in), deep purple bicolor.
'Langport Wren' AGM 56cm (22in), deep maroon self with brown beards.
'Magic Bubbles' AGM 61cm (24in), coral pink self.
'Mary Constance' AGM 63cm (25in), excellent ruffled deep violet-blue.
'Maui Moonlight' AGM 58cm (23in), lemon yellow self.
'Prince of Burgundy' AGM 56cm (22in), standards burgundy red, falls white with burgundy plicata edges. May rebloom. Sass Medal.
'Raspberry Blush' AGM 51cm (20in), tall, rich pink self, pink beards. Sass Medal.
'Strawberry Love' AGM 51cm (20in), Australian-bred rose pink bitone.
'Templecloud' AGM 61cm (24in), very pale blue standards, violet falls.
'Zing Me' 51cm (20in), cream/lemon, brown fall patches and beards.

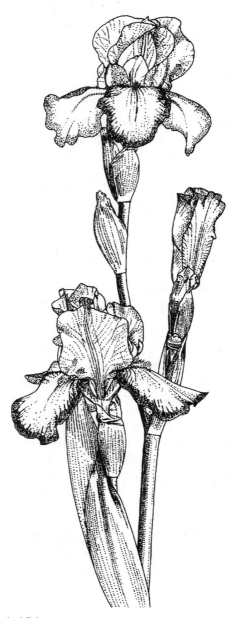

Intermediate Bearded Iris

MINIATURE TALL BEARDED (MTB) & BORDER BEARDED (BB) IRISES

Irises in these groups flower later than the IBs, in company with the Tall Beardeds, but provide variety by being shorter and are useful for planting in front of the talls, or in smaller gardens or spaces, or windy sites. They have the same height limits as the IBs but will probably have more flowers on each stem and should be cultivated as for the tall beardeds.

In the USA, MTBs are called 'Table Irises' because they are so well suited for flower arranging. Eight or more flowers, slightly smaller than those of IBs, are carried on each slender, graceful stem and breeders concentrate on maintaining their elegance, including that of the flowers. The plants may take a little longer than other beardeds to settle after planting and should be kept just moist until growing away satisfactorily. As a fairly recent development, there are fewer of them around but they are steadily increasing in number and availability. Some suggestions are:

'Bumblebee Deelite' AGM 45cm (18in), yellow, with large, deep maroon areas on the falls. Williamson-White Medal (AIS).

'Carolyn Rose' AGM 58cm (23in), fine pink plicating on a white ground.

'Chickee' AGM 48cm (19in), pure medium yellow self.

'Lady Belle' AGM 56cm (22in), standards white with purple-shaded bases, falls white with purple stitching.

'Loose Valley' 56cm (22in), standards maize yellow, falls cream, maize edges with faint purple plicating. AGM recommended, to be confirmed when this cultivar is in commerce (which should be quite soon).

'New Idea' 66cm (26in), a rosy mulberry self with yellow beard. Williamson-White Medal.

'Robin Goodfellow' AGM 48cm (19in), pure white self, very vigorous and free-flowering.

'Welch's Reward' AGM 56cm (22in), yellow standards, red-purple falls with yellow edgings.

The Border Beardeds have the same height limits as the MTBs and also flower along with them and with the Tall Beardeds but they have thicker stems and larger flowers than the MTBs. This may make them sound inelegant but with the flowers being in proportion to their height they are an attractive addition to the bearded cultivars and very suitable for planting in front of the talls. **'Orinoco Flow'** is a British-bred BB, a deep violet on white plicata, which has proven to be an outstanding 'doer' overseas as well as in its own country where it has an AGM and also won the Dykes Medal. In the USA, the only median ever to win the Dykes Medal is **'Brown Lasso'** which has butterscotch standards and violet falls with brown edges; it has also been given the AGM in RHS trials. Listed below are some other reliable cultivars.

'**Apricot Frosty**' 58cm (23in), white standards and apricot falls. AIS Knowlton Medal winner.

'**Batik**' 66cm (26in), a 'streaked' pattern of deep purple on white.

'**Blackbeard**' AGM 64cm (25in), pale steel blue, striking purple/black beard.

Cool Treat' AGM 66cm (26in), amoena, white standards and blue-violet falls.

'**Cranapple**' AGM 61cm (24in), cranberry bicolor, falls deeper than standards. Knowlton Medal.

'**Jungle Shadows**' 66cm (26in), brown/grey/purple blend. Knowlton Medal.

'**Pink Bubbles**' 56cm (22in), light pink self. Knowlton Medal.

'**Raspberry Sundae**' 66cm (26in), mulberry-rose self. Knowlton Medal.

'**Whoop 'em Up**' 69cm (27in), gold standards, falls maroon, edged gold. Knowlton Medal.

TALL BEARDED (TB) IRISES

These are amongst the best known of irises, not least because of their size and glamorous appearance. But while there are historic cultivars, even some survivors from the 19th century that keep growing and flowering with minimal attention (but well repay better treatment), the range of colours of modern TBs is far wider. The other big point in their favour is that the flowers are bred with much stronger substance and stand up to adverse weather far better, being unlikely to collapse into crumpled, mushy heaps in wind and rain. They can be damaged, of course, in really nasty spells but as most will carry at least eight buds and maybe up to twelve (old cultivars usually manage fewer than this) on several branches, there will probably be undamaged ones to open later. The number of flowers per stem means that an established clump with numerous stems will be in bloom for 3 to 4 weeks, in which they compare well with other exciting perennials such as peonies and oriental poppies. Plants that flower for months can be the backbone of the garden, but few have quite the same dramatic impact.

Any bearded iris over 71cm (28in) in height is classified as a TB though the majority are around 91cm (3ft) which brings the flowers to a comfortable height for close inspection, something worth trying as there is not only the overall impact of the large flowers but often great subtleties of colouring, light and shadows.

It must be admitted than TBs may not be the best of mixers, as their height fits them for further back in the border but their need for sun limits the plants that can be grown around them. This can be dealt with in several ways: a 'promontory' of TBs coming forward at intervals, or a 'bay' of not too vigorous carpeters in front of them. Or they can have a bed of their own, and some companions to provide colour at other times were suggested on page 14. New plants should be set about 30-38cm (12-15in) apart as they will need space to expand but annuals, or bulbs for permanence, will fit between them. This is advice for climates like Britain's; where summers are hotter and drier some shade, from overhead or from surrounding plants, may be desirable. The best time for planting is fairly soon after flowering ends when new roots are beginning to grow, though if new plants, either in containers or bare-rooted, are available at other times they should be set out as soon as possible providing weather and other conditions allow. After three to four years it will probably be necessary to lift and replant sizeable clumps, keeping the best rhizomes and discarding spent or weak ones. Leaves should be trimmed and plants temporarily staked if necessary to prevent wind-rock until the roots have good anchorage. If a single rhizome flowers in the first year after planting it may also need staking, especially in a windy site, and it is worth doing this to help the plant become well established. The suggested top-dressing should be applied at 75g per m^2 (2½ oz per yd^2).

There is a steady trend towards irises that bloom more than once a year, called remontants or repeat bloomers. They need some extra attention: a second feed after their first blooming and watering in dry spells, as they need to make faster growth. Not all can be relied on to rebloom in all climates, especially cooler ones, but the number and range is increasing and they are well worth trying. The IB **'Prince of Burgundy'** is a remontant median and some TBs are included in the list of suggestions below. 'Space Age' irises, another modern development, have been mentioned; some will be found in the list, and there are shorter ones such as SDB **'Stinger'** AGM, with yellow standards, yellow and white falls stitched with violet, and orange beards with purple horns.

'Alien Mist' 94cm (37in), palest blue self, blue-violet beards and horns
'Annabel Jane' 1.22m (48in), lilac bitone. British Dykes Medal.
'Beverly Sills' 91cm (36in), coral pink, tangerine beard. AIS Dykes Medal.
'Bob Nichol' AGM 91cm (36in), buttercup yellow self.
'Breakers' AGM 94cm (37in), ruffled blue self. May rebloom.
'Cardew' AGM 1m (39in), pale blue standards, red-violet falls.
'Charger' 73cm (29in), deep red self.
'Champagne Elegance' 84cm (33in), white and buff. May rebloom.
'Conjuration' 91cm (36in), white with blue edges, red beards, white horns. DM, USA.
'Dark Rosaleen' AGM 78cm (31in), red-black. May rebloom.
'Designer's Choice' AGM 81cm (32in), white self.
'Dutch Chocolate' 89cm (35in), reddish chocolate self. May rebloom.
'Dwight Enys' AGM 86cm (34in), yellow standards, red-brown falls.

'**Earl of Essex**' 89cm (35in), white and orchid/violet plicata. May rebloom.
'**Early Light**' AGM 97cm (38in), creamy yellow bitone. British DM.
'**Edith Wolford**' 1.02m (40in), yellow standards, blue-violet falls. DM, USA.
'**Feu du Ciel**' 89cm (35in), bright orange self.
'**Golden Encore**' 89cm (35in), golden yellow, white fall centre. Older but quite reliable remontant.
'**Jane Phillips**' AGM 91cm (36in), still very popular light blue self.
'**Kent Pride**' 75cm (30in), chestnut standards, falls yellow and white with chestnut plicata marks, another popular older cultivar.
'**Lark Rise**' AGM 97cm (38in), grey-blue standards, deep lavender falls.
'**Mesmerizer**' 91cm (36in), white, tangerine beards with white flounces and pale green pompons. DM, USA.
'**Night Owl**' 97cm (38in), purple-black self, black beard, velvety falls.
'**Olympic Torch**' 97cm (38in), light golden-bronze self.
'**Princess Sabra**' AGM 97cm (38in), shot pink standards, burgundy falls.
'**Repartee**' 75cm (30in), white standards, red falls. May rebloom.
'**Silverado**' 97cm (38in), butterfly blue self. DM, USA.
'**Sky Hooks**' 97cm (38in), soft yellow, golden beards, violet horns.
'**Snowy Owl**' AGM 97cm (38in), pure white self, including the beards.
'**Stepping Out**' AGM 97cm (38in), deep purple on white plicata. DM, USA.
'**Superstition**' AGM 91cm (36in), dark reddish-black self.
'**Thornbird**' AGM 89cm (35in), pale ecru/brownish-tan bicolor, small violet horns or spoons. DM, USA.
'**Titan's Glory**' AGM 94cm (37in), bishop's purple self. DM, USA.
'**Vanity**' AGM 91cm (36in), pink self. DM, USA.
'**Wensleydale**' AGM 1.0m (40in), white standards tinted violet, violet falls. British DM.

SOME BEARDED IRIS SPECIES

Pogoniris species are the ancestors of the huge number of cultivars and are well worth growing in their own right, though as they hail from a variety of locations not all will grow in every garden. In general they need the same conditions and cultivation as cultivars of similar size, with more tender ones having special treatment, such as protection in winter, in cooler situations.

Iris germanica AGM, whose name is often used incorrectly to cover Tall Bearded cultivars, is of uncertain origin and may not be a true species but the 'old blue flag' is a tough garden plant which may rebloom. Deep violet, about 75cm (30in) tall, it has a number of forms: *I.* '**Florentina**' AGM, 40cm (16in), with whitish flowers, was once a source of orris root, but until recently *I. pallida* AGM was the iris most widely grown in Italy for its rhizomes, which were harvested and dried to yield orris powder for perfumery and other uses. Sadly, synthetic alternatives are now mostly preferred but Chianti wine is still flavoured with orris. The iris itself is an excellent garden one, its light violet-blue, scented flowers borne on 60-91cm (2-3ft) stems and its blue-green foliage an asset for many months. *I.p.* 'Variegata' AGM has the same good flowers and decorative foliage striped lengthwise with yellow, while *I.p.* 'Argentea Variegata' with white stripes is less vigorous and tends to produce poor flowers. *I. variegata* AGM with yellow standards and reddish brown falls has set the name for the 'variegata' colour pattern in bearded cultivars. Its form *reginae* is white with many violet veins and of similar height, 40-50cm (16-20in). *I. albicans,* white, is another of IB height, often found on graves in Muslim countries.

Dwarf and median Pogon cultivars were originally developed from several delightful species. Like their descendants, the species can exhaust the soil around their short roots and need replanting more frequently than taller beardeds. *Iris aphylla* is purple and varies in height from 15-45cm (6-18in), with taller forms having branches and more flowers. Also variable is *I. lutescens* AGM (syn. *I. chamaeiris),* 8-25cm (3-10in), in yellow, purple or white. *I. reichenbachii,* yellow or brownish purple, and *I. schachtii,* similar and with a good purple form, are both 18cm (7in) tall.

Iris pumila is another misapplied name when used for Dwarf Bearded cultivars. The species is 8-13cm (3-5in) tall and can be violet-purple, yellow, white, blue or black. Two other tinies which are safer in a bulb frame or cold greenhouse are *I. suaveolens* (syn. *I. mellita),* violet, crimson or yellowish, and purple *I. attica.* Slugs, snails and too much wet are their enemies in the open.

This is a small selection of species that are relatively undemanding. Others may be available but it is as well to know if they have particular requirements. The most comprehensive book is *A Guide to Species Irises* (see p. 60 for details), or there is information in books on irises or perennials.

ARIL IRISES

These are the most exotic bearded irises but it is not easy to grow them in climates such as the British one, as most need thorough baking in summer, moisture in autumn and spring, and more or less dry winters, probably under a blanket of snow - though not all are cold-hardy. They are distinguished by having arils on their seeds and of the five sections into which the species are divided, *Oncocyclus* and *Regelia* are the best known though some others, particularly Pseudoregelias, are in cultivation. With some exceptions they are really for the specialist except in parts of the world where the conditions they need occur naturally - parts of the USA such as New Mexico, and South Australia, for example. The alternative is to grow them under glass and there is information later in this booklet. *A Guide to Species Irises* is also very helpful. One *Regelia* species, **Iris hoogiana**, can be grown outside in warm dry areas of Britain if drainage is excellent and it is given overhead cover such as a sheet of glass after flowering, if the summer is damp and cool. It has pale lavender flowers and is up to 66cm (26in) tall. *I.h.* **'Alba'** is white-flowered and the hybrid **'Bronze Beauty'** a brown bitone. They increase by stolons as does *I. stolonifera* and its cultivars, reddish brown **'Vera'** which has a blue beard, and **'Zwanenburg Beauty'**, pale mauve with reddish streaks, all quite easy to grow. Other possibilities are the *Regelio-cyclus*, hybrids between the *Oncocyclus* and *Regelia* Sections around 30-40cm (12-16in) tall, such as **'Chione'**, white with blue/grey veins and a dark patch on the falls; **'Clotho'**, deep violet and black, and **'Dardanus'**, lilac standards and cream falls with purple veining.

Hybrids between bearded iris cultivars and aril irises, Arilbreds, are a slightly easier proposition, though the amount of aril blood can vary and affect the conditions they need: those with the most, half or three-quarters aril, are usually safest under glass but the one-quarter arils may well be happy outside in a suitable spot. **'Lady Mohr'** is an old but reliable hybrid, 75cm (30in) tall, pale lavender and yellow with crimson markings and a brown beard. There is a good selection from specialist suppliers in the USA, and some newer American Arilbreds available in Britain include **'Bionic Comet'**, 61cm (24in) tall, old gold with maroon signal and beard (a feature of *Oncocyclus* irises, a dark signal patch on the falls, is quite often passed on to Arilbreds); **'Desert Dream'**, violet to violet-grey, black beard, 66cm (26in) tall; and **'Prophetic Message'**, 51cm (20in), with violet standards and falls a blend of violet and brown, and bronze beards. Some British-bred arilbreds were listed in *The RHS Plant Finder* fairly recently and might be available again. Among them were **'Main Sequence'**, 71cm (28in), yellow with maroon signals and yellow beards; **'Windrider'**, 78cm (31in), pale blue standards and pale violet falls, maroon signals and orange beards; and **'Wine and Lilac'**, 75cm (30in), lilac standards, lilac-rose falls, burgundy signals, purple beards.

Beardless Irises

THESE ARE THE APOGONS OR SUBGENUS *LIMNIRIS*, a very diverse group but almost all good for combining with other plants. The majority of those described below are hardy but some cannot be grown in very dry climates; some will grow in places that are partly shaded while others need plenty of sun. Most of the sections contain both species and cultivars. There are well-known groups such as the Siberians, Pacific Coast, Japanese, Series *Spuriae* and water irises, the *Unguiculares* and *Iris foetidissima*, plus the Evansias, which have crests in place of beards, and some lesser-known irises well worth growing.

Advice as to siting and cultivation will be found for each group, as their needs, though usually easy to satisfy, are so variable.

THE CRESTED IRISES

Recent DNA investigations may result in some of the irises in this group being re-classified but that will be in the future. These are the Evansias, Section *Lophiris*, some of which have flowers often mistaken for orchids, all of them with a ridged crest on the falls where bearded irises have beards. The rhizomes may grow horizontally on the surface of the soil, perhaps spreading by stolons, but other species have vertical green 'canes' that function as rhizomes. Heights range from very tiny to over two metres and while some are hardy, others need sheltered positions or to be grown under glass except in warmer regions.

Two North American natives, which can take some shade especially where summers are fairly hot at times, are **Iris cristata** and **I. lacustris,** both of which have the RHS AGM. They are stoloniferous and have violet-blue flowers with orange or yellow crests, seen in late spring. A neutral or lime-free soil with plenty of humus is what they need and they do well in the rock garden, troughs and pots, but should be divided and replanted every two to three years like other small irises. *I. lacustris* is only 2-5cm (1-2in) tall and can be less easy to keep than *I. cristata* which reaches 10cm (4in). **I. c. 'Alba'** is a very pretty white and other colour forms are known in the USA. A good hybrid between the two species has lavender flowers.

The third small Evansia is **Iris gracilipes,** native to Asia. It has slender, branched stems 10-15cm (4-6in) tall with several dainty flowers, lilac-mauve, or white in **I.g. 'Alba'**, and needs similar conditions to the North American pair, making a charming plant for places that are not too hot. It has been hybridized with *I. lacustris.* All the above have horizontal rhizomes and are deciduous. The same applies to two other species but they are much larger and more substantial plants that need sunny positions in well-drained but rich soil; they are heavy feeders and as well as having good nourishment dug in before planting they require top-dressing twice a year with 2cm (1in) of well-rotted compost. This should be given in spring and again after flowering ends. Both are moderately cold-hardy but cannot survive in wet soils. The taller is *Iris milesii* AGM with many lilac-pink flowers with darker markings and gold crests on much branched stems up to 91cm (36in) tall, in early summer. *Iris tectorum* is the 'roof iris' of Japan, where it was seen growing on thatched roofs, but it was probably introduced from China long ago. Its stems are around 30cm (12in) tall, carrying large violet-blue flowers with white crests and there is also a fine white form. The broad, glossy leaves catch the light attractively, and there is a very rare variegated form (most offered under this name are in fact *I. japonica* 'Variegata').

With short roots, *I. tectorum* quickly exhausts the soil around it and should be replanted every other year soon after flowering in early summer as well as being top-dressed twice yearly. Slightly less hardy than *I. milesii*, it does better in a sheltered spot, or makes a good pot plant if well fed. *I.* **'Paltec'** is a hybrid of *I. pallida* and *I. tectorum* which can be grown in a warm spot like a bearded iris and has silvery-blue flowers.

The evergreen, 'cane' Evansias are less hardy and some can only be grown under glass except in warm climates. At the tops of green, rather bamboo-like, thick stems - the canes - are fans of glossy leaves. The hardiest is *Iris japonica*, often sold as *I.j.* **'Ledger's Variety'**, reputed to be hardier than the type, and this can be grown out of doors in sunny, well-drained places with some shelter or in warm gardens. As well as canes this species has horizontal green rhizomes and the frilly white flowers, prettily marked in violet and orange, appear on much branched stems up to 1m (39in) tall. *I.j.* **'Variegata'**, and *I.j.* **'Aphrodite'**, have leaves striped with pale cream and flower less freely in cooler areas. *I.j.* **'Bourne Graceful'** is a delightful hybrid between two forms of *I. japonica*, with very pale mauve flowers. Grow them all in good soil and mulch as for *I. milesii;* they all do well in pots.

Iris confusa AGM can be tried outside; it needs a frost-free, well-drained site in a fairly dry and warm area, conditions that can be provided in parts of Britain, but it is really safer under glass as it is definitely less hardy than the Evansias described above. Green canes, from 30 to 80cm (12-32in) tall, arise from the roots and branched stems bearing ruffled white flowers with orange-yellow crests and markings emerge from fans of leaves at the tips of the canes. *I.c.* **'Martyn Rix'**, a collected form that may be hardier as it seems to prefer cooler conditions without direct sun, has blue-violet flowers.

Iris japonica

SERIES *UNGUICULARES*

There are two species in this Series, winter-flowering irises of which the best known is ***Iris unguicularis*** AGM. This is a much loved plant where and when it performs well, producing a succession of lavender-blue blooms over several months. When milder weather allows the buds to develop, they appear and open very quickly, as long as the site has some shelter - a wall behind it facing south or thereabouts is a help - and is very well drained and preferably slightly alkaline. It is better left undisturbed if possible to develop into a sizeable clump with a multitude of flowers - a lovely sight. That is the ideal but even given the best conditions there is no certainty of getting such a reward. This can also be the most frustrating of irises, blooming sparsely or not at all, and the answer may not be easy to find. Heavy feeding only produces leaves that shade the rhizomes, depriving them of essential baking and ripening in summer, so apply only a little general fertiliser that is not too high in nitrogen from time to time, or dig it in before planting. A clump of several rhizomes is easier to establish than a small piece and it should be planted with the rhizomes at the soil surface and kept just moist until growing away, in a sunny spot and not shaded by other plants. The foliage itself may give too much shade but it can be trimmed back to 15cm (6in) or so in summer, while dead leaves should be gently removed at any time. Being evergreen, it is not, alas, a plant for areas with harsh winters.

Iris unguicularis

The flowers are carried on long perianth tubes with the ovaries below them on a tiny true stem. It is easy to miss seedpods, so close to the ground and among leaves. A good way to enjoy the scent is to pull the buds gently at the base of the tubes and put them in water indoors, but watch for slugs and snails who will try to get to them first. Birds sometimes peck the flowers for the nectar.

There are larger, pale lilac flowers on *I.u.* **'Walter Butt'**, which is well scented and often one of the earliest to flower. A vigorous clone with typical flowers is *I.u* **'Marondera'** and there are various colour forms. White ones vary in vigour and flower quality and there are lavender pinks and several with flowers striped in lavender, purple and white, such as *I.u.*

'Kilndown'. Deep violet and usually free-flowering, *I.u.* **'Mary Barnard'** AGM has narrow leaves, and does not seem to need as much shelter (even overhead protection in wet winters) as *I.u.* subsp. *cretensis*, *I.u.* subsp. *carica* var. *angustifolia*, and *I.u.* **'Abington Purple'**.

The second species, less well known than it should be, is *Iris lazica* AGM. Coming from around the Black Sea and damper, shadier places than those in North Africa and Greece, which are home to *I. unguicularis*, it performs reliably in cooler gardens as well as warmer ones though it should not be baked. Evergreen, with broader, brighter green foliage, its flowers range from lavender to dark purple and often begin in late autumn. In Britain, *I.l.* **'Joy Bishop'** is a good new clone with redder-toned flowers.

PACIFIC COAST IRISES (PCIs)

These delightful plants, with jewel-like flowers in almost all iris colours, are mostly evergreen, which sadly makes them less than hardy in regions with very cold winters. They are often called Californians, indeed are Series *Californicae*, but are found, usually in mountainous areas and at the edges of woodland, from California northwards through Oregon and Washington. Those from the southern end of their range are less cold-hardy and may not survive British winters. Nevertheless, if they can be grown (and the majority of hybrids and cultivars *are* hardy), they should be in every garden where the soil is neutral or mildly acid and make attractive companions for perennials other than thugs, or ground cover around ericaceous shrubs. In cool gardens they flower better if there is sun for a good part of the day, provided they never get too dry, but in warmer situations some shade is appreciated, even necessary. Dig in plenty of humus, good compost or leaf mould (as long as it is not alkaline), to produce soil that is moisture-retentive but never waterlogged, and mulch the plants lightly with the same. Planting is best done in early autumn and if plants are being divided, split them into small clumps, not single rhizomes. Never let the roots get dry; wrap them in a damp covering or stand them in shallow water temporarily, then plant the small woody rhizomes about 2.5cm (1in) deep, and keep them well watered until they are growing away. They can be grown in pots where garden conditions are unsuitable but should not get pot-bound.

There are good ranges of named cultivars available in the USA and elsewhere but raising plants from seed mixtures should produce an assortment of colours and patterns and is easy if a little extra care is taken. Space the seeds well apart in pots of lime-free compost, with a light covering of compost or grit, and plunge the pots in a frame or open space with some shading. When the seedlings have five leaves each plant in their permanent places, in spring or autumn, with the minimum of root disturbance and keep them nicely moist. Or they can be potted singly until their places, or the weather, are suitable for planting out.

Among the species, *Iris douglasiana* AGM is exceptional as it will tolerate a little lime. Its somewhat lax, branched stems are up to 70cm (28in) long with three to nine flowers, most often lavender though they can be from red-purple through to white. The evergreen leaves are long, too, perhaps with red bases. *I.d.* **'Agnes James'** AGM is a very fine collected form, with white flowers veined in gold.

Iris innominata, another evergreen, has finer, shorter leaves and an upright habit, with two flowers per 15-25cm (6-10in) stem. These are often yellow but may be blue, lilac, purple, orange or cream, with pretty veining.

Similar in size are *I. thompsonii,* blue to purple, and *I. tenax,* which is usually deciduous and comes in purple, lavender or creamy yellow.

Slightly taller are *I. bracteata,* yellow, and *I. purdyi,* cream with pink or purple veins, both 20-30cm (8-12in) tall and with small leaves on their stems.

Beautiful shades of blue occur in *I. macrosiphon* and *I. munzii,* but the first is slightly less hardy than those above and the second is quite tender. As the species interbreed readily when growing near each other, hybrids frequently occur and it may be quite difficult to get true species.

Some good British-bred cultivars are:

'Arnold Sunrise' AGM 25cm (10in), white with blue shading and orange centres on the falls.

'Banbury Beauty' AGM, 54cm (21in), lavender, purple signal. Also other PCIs with the 'Banbury' prefix.

'Blue Ballerina' AGM 38cm (15in), near white with black and purple signal.

'Broadleigh Carolyn' AGM 45cm (18in), pale blue with deeper veining and purple signal, and other 'Broadleigh' cultivars.

'Goring Ace' AGM 25cm (10in), gold, crimson veins and edges.

'Little Tilgates' AGM 30cm (12in), peach self, radiant centre.

'No Name' AGM 30cm (12in,) bright yellow. The only PCI to have won the Dykes Medal.

'Pinewood Amethyst' 30cm (12in), amethyst self.

Hybrids between the Californicae and the Sino-Siberians are called Cal-sibs. One of the first was red-purple **'Margot Holmes'**, bred by Amos Perry, which won the first ever British Dykes Medal in 1927 and is still offered. Several hybridisers are working on this group, in the USA and Germany particularly, and new hybrids in many colours are being bred. Older, still reliable, ones such as **'Fine Line'** AGM, pale yellow with many purple veins, a cinnamon pink effect, 48cm (19in), **'Golden Waves'** light yellow 61cm (24in), and **'Wise Gift'** AGM, deep violet, 55cm (22in), are sterile diploids. Tetraploids, which should be fertile, are increasingly available: in Britain they include **'Goring Steeple'** AGM, 72cm (28in) tall, yellow, rose and purple.

SIBERIAN IRISES

This is the garden name for a well-known, deservedly popular, group belonging to Series *Sibiricae* but is a little misleading. Linnaeus named *Iris sibirica* AGM thinking it to be a native of Siberia but it reaches no nearer than Russia and spreads westward to central Europe. *Iris sanguinea* AGM (formerly *I. orientalis* of Miller) is a close relative that grows in Siberia and parts of the Far East, while from China there is *I. typhifolia*, only brought into cultivation in the west quite recently. Nevertheless, Siberian Irises is a convenient name for these species and the cultivars descended from hybrids between them.

All have narrow, rather grassy, deciduous green leaves, those of *Iris typhifolia* being the narrowest. The tallest stems are seen in *I. sibirica*, up to 91cm (36in) and branched with up to ten smallish, blue-violet and white, fluttering flowers. *Iris sanguinea* is the shortest, around 75cm (30in), with two larger dark violet flowers per stem, and reddish spathes covering the ovaries. Both species have white forms but they are rather confused, not least because they interbreed very readily. *Iris typhifolia* is intermediate in height and size of bloom, usually with blue-violet flowers though with some variation, which appear earlier than those of the other species, in late spring. It may rebloom, but seems to flower less well in cooler places.

Any soil which is not too acid or too alkaline is suitable. It should be able to retain some moisture although when clumps are well established most will stand periods of drought if not too prolonged; *Iris typhifolia* may perhaps do better in slightly damper soil, but none of the species or cultivars will tolerate being waterlogged. Though all need some sun to flower well, and generally prefer open positions, some shade may be welcome in places with hot summers. Clumps of three, four or more rhizomes should be planted about 2-5cm (1-2in) deep, with compost or manure dug in first and used as a light mulch later, and slow-release general fertiliser seems to benefit them. Division and transplanting can be done soon after flowering ends, or be delayed until early autumn. Water the newly planted pieces thoroughly and keep them moist. Unless the dead leaves are needed for protection in places with cold winters, cut them off when they die back or slugs and snails will find homes from which to attack the new shoots in spring.

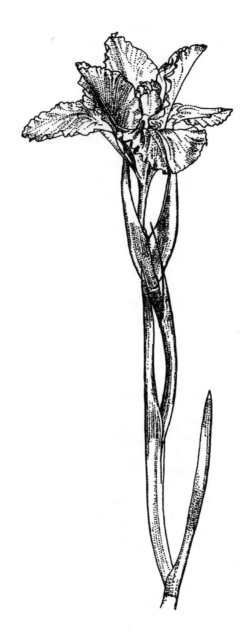

Pacific Coast Iris cultivar

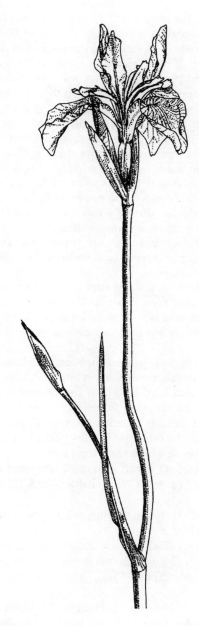

Iris sibirica cultivar

Most cultivars have *Iris sibirica* and *I. sanguinea* and hybrids between them as ancestors but *I. typhifolia* is now contributing its particular qualities. The number of named cultivars is steadily increasing as is the colour range, which includes all shades of blue, violet and purple, lavender, lilac, wine-red and white. Yellow and pink are more recent developments and flowers often combine two or more colours, especially in the style arms. Signals can be very decorative and there may be white or golden edges to falls, sometimes standards too. Historic cultivars have forms similar to those of the species, with rather hanging falls, and though hybridisers have been working for, and getting, more flaring shapes there is also recognition that 'vertical' form has garden value. There are dwarf forms of the two main species as well as some cultivars, in heights from 15-45cm (6-18in).

Tetraploid cultivars have twice the normal number of chromosomes. The first ones were induced through the use of colchicine and then interbred to develop a race that has stronger substance in flowers and leaves and can be more vigorous than diploids. From the gardener's angle, knowing whether a cultivar is diploid or tetraploid may not matter much, but it is important to hybridisers.

Repeat-blooming cultivars usually start earlier than the rest and then begin again a few weeks after their first period of bloom ends, though some do not rebloom until late summer or early autumn. They need sufficient, though not too much, summer warmth and adequate moisture in order to develop further flowers.

Seedlings are generally easy to raise and can be planted out when the leaves are 15cm (6in) or so tall, though if it is late in the season they may be safer potted individually and kept in a cold frame until spring. Seed from mixed cultivars should give a variety of forms and colours.

It can almost be said that any Siberian iris is worth garden space, and choosing from so many can be difficult. The list below is just a selection of good ones. (T) indicates those which are tetraploids

'Baby Sister' 15-22cm (6-9in), dwarf with quite large mid-blue flowers.

'Berlin Ruffles' AGM (T) 1m (39in), ruffled mid blue. Dykes Medal (BIS).

'Butter and Sugar' AGM 68cm (27in), white standards, yellow falls. Morgan-Wood Medal (AIS).

'Caesar's Brother' 94cm (37in), historic deep violet self, sizeable flowers.

'Cambridge' AGM 86cm (34in), light violet-blue. Dykes Medal (BIS).

Dreaming Yellow' AGM 91cm (36in), white to creamy yellow. May rebloom.

'Exuberant Encore' (T) 35-81cm (14-32in). Mid-blue repeater, short stems in first blooming, taller, branched ones later.

'**Glaslyn**' AGM (T) 97cm (38in), pale blue standards, darker falls.

'**Harpswell Happiness**' AGM (T) 75cm (30in), white self, yellow-green veins.

'**Helen Astor**' 75cm (30in), historic light wine-red, white signals.

'**Lady Vanessa**' 91cm (36in), wine-red bitone. Morgan-Wood Medal.

'**Mrs Rowe**' 61cm (24in), pale lilac, small-flowered historic cultivar.

'**Perfect Vision**' AGM (T) 86cm (34in), blue bitone, turquoise style arms. Dykes Medal (BIS).

'**Perry's Blue**' 91cm (36in), medium blue, historic, good cut flower.

'**Pink Haze**' 89cm (35in), pale lavender-pink standards, deeper falls. Morgan-Wood Medal.

'**Reprise**' AGM 81cm (32in), violet self, repeat bloomer.

'**Rosselline**' AGM 62cm (26in), lilac standards, red-violet falls.

'**Ruffled Velvet**' AGM 75cm (30in), red-purple, gold signal. Morgan Award (AIS)

'**Shirley Pope**' AGM 81cm (32in), very dark, velvety red-purple, white signal.

'**Silver Edge**' AGM (T) 91cm (36in), blue bitone, falls edged silvery-white. Morgan Award (AIS).

'**Soft Blue**' AGM 75cm (30in), light blue, vertical form, reliable repeat bloom in many parts of Britain and the USA.

'**White Swirl**' AGM 97cm (38in), older white self, flaring falls.

Hybrids between Siberian Iris cultivars and *Iris setosa*, known as Sibtosas, are good garden plants for dampish soil. Branched stems, 61-75cm (24-30in) tall, carry blue, violet or lavender-pink flowers.

SINO-SIBERIAN IRISES

Another group with a less than totally accurate but convenient name, these are irises native to China and westward to the Himalaya. Botanists include them in Series *Sibiricae* but they have a different chromosome number, slightly different appearance, and require rather damper soil than the Siberians though they are by no means water or bog plants. They are also less tolerant of lime in the soil and water but generally easy to grow and mix with other perennials in similar conditions.

An asset is that the flowers, though usually smaller than those of the Siberians, have a greater natural colour range as it includes yellow as well as blue, purple and red, and hybrids often include more than one of these colours and can be attractively veined and speckled. As they interbreed very readily true species are not always easy to obtain but species and hybrids are easily raised from seed with rewarding results. Planted with the rhizomes 2-5cm (1-2in) deep in well-prepared soil, and given good cultivation, plants can be long-lived but sometimes, and for no obvious reason, they may decline. Exhaustion of the soil, perhaps a lack of trace elements, may be a cause, especially with smaller plants with relatively short roots.

Iris chrysographes AGM is well known - another name for the whole group is Subseries *Chrysographes*, from this species - with variable flower colouring, from blue, through reddish-purple (**'Rubella'**) to deep red-purple or black. The specific name refers to the 'gold writing', marks in the signal area, though not all forms have it. It has fine grassy leaves and two flowers on each 35cm (14in) tall stem. Similar in size and appearance, *I. bulleyana* has blue-violet flowers, or a white form. Deep purple *I. delavayi* AGM is taller and huskier, up to 1.5m (5ft) tall with branched stems and more, larger flowers. *Iris clarkei* AGM is blue- to reddish-violet, with white signals, 61cm (24in) tall. The yellow-flowered species are *I. forrestii* and *I. wilsonii;* the first is only 15-40cm (6-16in) tall, with narrow leaves glossy green above, greyish beneath, and the second taller, 61-75cm (24-30in), and more vigorous but a paler yellow. Both have unbranched stems.

Specialist societies' seed lists usually offer seed of mixed hybrids, well worth a try. There are named cultivars to be found in Britain via *The RHS Plant Finder*, and very interesting hybridising is going on in Germany and the USA, especially in the Pacific North-West.

MOISTURE-LOVING IRISES

Series *Laevigatae* contains some irises that no garden should be without if there is a pond, a bog, or an area which is damp for much of the year, preferably with lime-free soil and high in humus. One of the loveliest of all irises is *Iris laevigata* AGM in its typical violet-blue form, a classic shape and an asset to even the smallest pool. The species and its cultivars do need to grow in shallow water such as at the edge of a pool, in 30cm (12in) of soil enriched with manure and with 5-8cm (2-3in) depth of water above the rhizomes. Stems around 61cm (24in) tall, with two to four flowers, appear in the later part of the main season, and **'Semperflorens'** may rebloom in early autumn.

Cultivars with upright, usually smallish, standards are known as 'singles'; they include *I.l.* **'Alba'**, white touched with pale violet, and the similar *I.l.* **'Weymouth Purity'**, deep wine-purple *I.l.* **'Atropurpurea'** and red-violet *I.l.* **'Regal'**. *I.l.* **'Weymouth Elegant'** has more extensive violet markings on a white ground. *I.l.* **'Variegata'** AGM has slightly paler violet-blue flowers than the type and beautiful green and white striped foliage that lasts all summer.

When the standards are enlarged and lie over and between the falls the flowers are called 'double'. Examples are pale blue *I.l.* **'Lilacina'**, darker in the centre, and *I.l.* **'Colchesterensis'** whose white petals have heavy deep violet mottling. *I.l.* **'Weymouth Midnight'** and *I.l.* **'Royal Cartwheel'** are very similar, both a striking very deep violet with six contrasting white central stripes.

The Yellow Flag, *Iris pseudacorus* AGM, native to Britain and throughout Europe and Asia to Japan, really needs a large pond or lake as it is so vigorous, but it is less rampant in a border that is fairly moist for most of the year. *I.p.* **'Variegata'** AGM, with lovely spring foliage striped in yellows and greens, grows more slowly and can be trusted in a smallish pond, but will also do well in moist soil. After producing typical golden-yellow flowers in midsummer the plant goes green all over, as does the pale yellow-leaved *I.p.* **'Lime Sorbet'**, but next spring's foliage will be typical again. Stem heights range from around 75cm (30in) in these forms, through 91cm (36in) or more of *I. pseudacorus*, to much taller forms such as *I.p.* **'Esk'** and *I.p.* **'Sun in Splendour'** (up to 1.68m/5½ft).

Paler-coloured forms include *I.p.* **'Alba'** (actually very pale cream) and slightly deeper ones with descriptive names - *I.p.* **'Ivory'**, *I.p.* **'Ecru'**, - and *I.p.* **'Turnipseed'**, which originated in an American nursery of that name, while. *I.p.* var *bastardii* is lemon-yellow. More cultivars, varying in colour and signal markings, are emerging in the USA. Two German tetraploids are *I.p.* **'Ilgengold'**, a bitone with paler standards, and deeper yellow *I.p.* **'Beuron'**; they are of sturdier build but not, overall, bigger than average. 'Double' forms, one flower growing from the centre of another, are *I.p.* **'Flore Pleno'** and *I.p.* **'Sun Cascade'**, and there are dwarfs, 50-70cm (20-28in) tall, with fewer flowers that may be rather low in the foliage.

The origins of **'Holden Clough'** AGM are mysterious, but it is a very good, not over-vigorous, relative of *Iris pseudacorus* with a yellow ground heavily veined with brown, and a parent of other good irises for moist soil. **'Berlin Tiger'**, **'Phil Edinger'** and **'Roy Davidson'** all have the AGM and are more or less densely veined in shades of brown on differing yellow backgrounds.

In North America there are no native yellow flags, but the blue flag, *Iris versicolor* AGM, is found from eastern Canada southwards to Texas and its relative *I. virginica* in the south-eastern USA. An excellent garden plant, *I. versicolor* will grow in any soil that is not too dry, very acid or alkaline, but does best in water or moist soil where it will grow to 61cm (24in) or more. Branched stems bear up to seven flowers, typically violet-blue but with natural variants including white *I.v.* **'Murrayana'**, pink (*I.v.* var.

rosea), purple, or wine-red in *I.v.* **'Kermesina'**. A range of cultivars raised in the USA includes *I.v.* **'Party Line'**, in two tones of pink, *I.v.* **'Pink Peaks'** with jagged tops to its standards, and whites with coloured veining, blue in *I.v.* **'Between the Lines'**, red in *I.v.* **'Mint Fresh'**, pinker in *I.v.* **'Candystriper'**. In Britain the *I.v.* **'Rowden'** cultivars have many colours and patterns. Dramatic *I.v.* **'Mysterious Monique'** from Germany is the darkest to date, with dark red standards, white style arms with red midribs, and velvety deep red-purple falls with gold and white signals.

Whilst *Iris versicolor* is completely cold-hardy, *I. virginica* is less so, though *I.v.* var. *shrevei* can be grown in Britain. Unbranched stems up to 91cm (36in) tall carry the lavender to violet flowers of *I. virginica,* whilst var. *shrevei* has branching stems and scented flowers.

Interesting hybrids among the moisture-loving irises are well worth garden space. *Iris pseudacorus* crossed with *I. versicolor* has produced several tall hybrids with violet veining on white grounds, such as **'Limbo'**. In **'Appointer'** the veining is redder and very dense while **'Regal Surprise'** is quite different; it has light reddish-violet standards, cream style arms and darker red-violet falls with yellow signals. In Japan, crossing *I. ensata* and *I. pseudacorus* resulted in cultivars with yellowish foliage and flowers, **'Aichi-no-kagayaki'** and **'Kinboshi'**, which are sterile and not very vigorous, but later efforts produced the stronger, fertile **'Hatsuho'** and the British-bred **'Chance Beauty'** which has bold yellow flowers with prominent chestnut markings and grows fast. Seedlings from it seem to be pure *I. pseudacorus* and if the seeds are wanted they should be collected as soon as the pods are ripe, as otherwise they fall into the parent clump and take it over. **Eye Shadow Irises** are later developments of such crosses, described under 'Japanese Irises'.

Versatas, Canadian-bred hybrids involving *Iris versicolor* and *I. ensata,* are other hybrids with lovely flowers for moist soil. In Britain it will be possible to see them, and others, in a trial at the RHS Wisley Gardens in 2003-5. **'Enfant Prodige'** has numerous flowers with lilac standards and large, deeper lilac falls on its 1.1m (43in) stems, **'Oriental Touch'** is somewhat similar and **'Violet Minuet'** is shorter with velvety falls setting off clear yellow signals. Hybrids between *I. versicolor* and *I. laevigata* such as **'Starting Versi-Laev'** can be grown in water, and for moist soil there are sibcolors, Siberian cultivars crossed with *I. versicolor.* There will surely be many more experiments in hybridising among the *Laevigatae* with equally worthwhile results.

SERIES *SPURIAE*

This Section contains plants suitable for sunny positions in good soil, mildly acid to mildly alkaline, with rotted manure or general fertiliser to nourish them, especially the taller ones. They will fit into a variety of places, the rock garden, front, middle or back of the border, according to their heights.

Generally, they do not like to get too dry for too long, and should be planted like most beardless irises, about 2-5cm (1-2in) deep, a little deeper in hotter climates. Most species are hardy, but the cultivars can vary according to where they were bred; those from the midwest of the USA being more cold-hardy than others which began life in California, for example. Most start to flower about the middle of the main season, some continuing into later weeks.

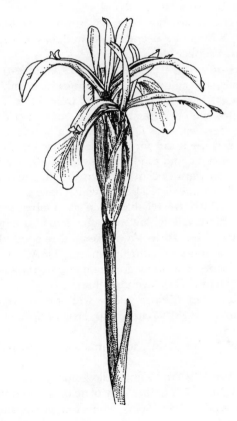

Iris kerneriana

Little *Iris graminea* AGM is usually the first. Only 15-20cm (6-8in) tall, its purple flowers smell of plums or greengages but *I.g.*var. *pseudocyperus,* which is taller, has no scent. Another for the rock garden, in spots which are not too dry, is *I. sintenisii* AGM which is a little shorter and has white flowers very densely veined with violet. Going up in height, a good border plant is yellow *Iris kerneriana* AGM, 20-40cm (8-16in) tall, but its nectar does attract ants (and no iris appreciates an ants' nest under its rhizomes). *Iris spuria* has several subspecies of different heights: *I.s.* subsp. *maritima* is 30cm (12in) tall with deep violet-blue falls and variably marked style arms. Style arms are prominent in the spurias, lying over the long hafts of the falls, which have relatively small, often nearly circular, blades. *I.s.* subsp. *sogdiana* is up to 50cm (20in), pale blue to lilac, *I.s.* subsp. *spuria* is similar in height but violet-blue. Creamy yellow *I.s.* subsp. *halophila* can be from 40 to 91cm (16-36in). Three taller subspecies, 90cm-1m (36-39in), are sky blue *I.s.* subsp. *carthaliniae*; *I.s.* subsp. *notha* that is a brighter, deeper blue and has a white form; and *I.s. musulmanica,* a similar blue.

Iris orientalis* AGM of Miller (syn *I. ochroleuca*), white with yellow signals on its falls, and soft yellow *I. monnieri* are both around 1m (39in). *Iris crocea* AGM (syn. *I. aurea*) reaches from 91 to 1.5m (3-5ft) and its golden yellow flowers, on a sizeable clump, make a striking addition to the back of the border, with the foliage giving a strong vertical accent. Two flowers per stem is the norm for the little spurias but the number increases according to the height, and modern cultivars can flower for several weeks.

Those bred in warmer climates than Britain's may not flower too well here, but as well as some, listed below, which have proved themselves, there are old hybrids which are reliable, such as **'Ochraurea'** and **'Shelford Giant'** AGM, both yellow-flowered, the latter around 2m. (6ft+) tall. **'Monspur Cambridge Blue'** AGM is another good old hybrid. There is a wide choice of modern cultivars in the USA, to be obtained from specialist iris nurseries, and some are being imported by British nurseries.

'Belise' AGM 94cm (37in), lavender blue.

'Cherokee Lace' 1m (39in), yellow with brown veining. British-bred.

'Clarke Cosgrove' AGM 97cm (38in), lavender, small yellow signal. Nies Award (AIS).

'Dawn Candle' 1.22m (48in), standards white, falls yellow, orange signal. Nies Award.

'Destination' AGM 1.02m (40in), yellow-orange self.

'Driftwood' AGM 1.37m (54in), chocolate brown and yellow.

'Ila Crawford' AGM 91cm (36in), white, orange signal.

'Janice Chesnik' 1.22-1.52m (48-60in), ruffled tawny gold self. Nies Award.

'Marilyn Holloway' 97cm (38in), pale lavender standards, falls yellow, edged with lavender.

'Missouri Rivers' 97cm (38in), ruffled blue, yellow signal. Nies Medal (AIS).

'Protégé' AGM 91cm (36in), blue standards, white falls veined blue.

'Sunrise in Sonora' AGM 1.12cm (44in), dark maroon violet, yellow blaze on falls.

JAPANESE IRISES (JIs)

Like the other moisture-loving irises, these belong to Series *Laevigatae* but, while most of those can be grown in water, Japanese Irises will not tolerate being waterlogged for long. *Iris ensata* AGM, the species from which a wide range of cultivars has been developed over centuries in Japan, inhabits northern China and eastern Siberia too. Formerly named *I. kaempferi*, it does grow in wet places but they tend to dry out in summer and the spectacular mass plantings of cultivars in public places which are flooded at flowering time in Japan to increase their effect have led to the erroneous idea that they are water plants. Certainly they do need moist soil and can be planted at the side of a pond but the crowns should be above water level, and they will do as well in a bed that does not dry out, in acid soil with composted farmyard manure added. A very few can tolerate slightly alkaline conditions but the majority will not, nor should they be irrigated with alkaline water. They do, however, take quite well to pot culture in ericaceous compost with added manure and rainwater used on them, or can be planted in a plastic-lined bed into which groundwater cannot penetrate. Make small holes in the base for drainage and watch for any yellowing of the leaves.

Tall, narrow standards, and broad hanging falls in red-purple, are typical of the wild *Iris ensata* but there are natural blue-purple, pink and white, and white variants. These were collected and grown in gardens and known as Nagai types from the region where they grew. Other flower forms evolved from them, **Edo** with horizontal falls, **Ise** with papery pendant falls which were used for pot culture, and **Higo**, a robust strain descended from Edo irises which were the ancestors of modern cultivars bred in Japan (where they are called Hanashobu) the USA and elsewhere.

The colours are still based on the original and its variants, though there is a great range of tones, combinations and patterns. Flower form can be very different from that of the species. There are '6-fall' or 'double' cultivars with enlarged standards lying more or less horizontally between the falls, and in 'paeony-flowered' JIs the style arms are much larger and more petaloid. Flowers can be large, up to 20cm (8in) across. It may be best to see them in flower or in photographs before buying as individual preferences will govern the choice. There are specialist nurseries, and others include reliable JIs among their lists of perennials.

The species and some cultivars have branching stems with four or more flowers, others have only two terminal blooms. Heights are mostly from 61 to 102cm (24-41in). Leaves should be a fresh green, with a pronounced midrib, or grey-green with white lengthwise stripes in *I.e.* **'Variegata'** AGM. Tetraploid cultivars, first developed in the USA, have thicker substance in their petals but are similar in size to diploids. There are repeat-blooming cultivars but they are most successful in areas with warm summers, and need extra feeding and water.

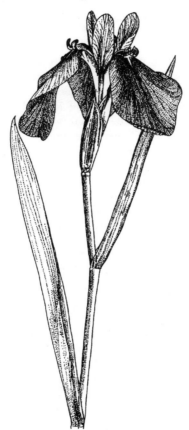

Iris ensata 'Variegata'

Some JIs which can be suggested for Britain are:

Single (3-fall) cultivars:
'**Alba**' 75cm (30in), white self.
'**Aldridge Prelude**' 91cm (36in), rosy lilac standards, violet falls, white and yellow signals.
'**Barr Purple East**' AGM 1.2m (48in), purple-violet bitone, darker veins, yellow signals.
'**Imperial Magic**' AGM 1.15m (46in), lilac standards edged in white, white falls with purple markings.
'**Returning Tide**' AGM 1.02m (41in), standards violet-blue, lighter falls. May rebloom. Payne Award (AIS).
'**Rose Queen**' AGM 97cm (38in), rose-pink self, close to species in form.
'**Rowden King**' 91cm (36in), deep red-purple standards, pinkish-mauve falls, white style arms. Can tolerate a little lime.
'**Rowden Mikado**' 91cm (36in), standards and styles deep purple and white, falls white overlaid purple, blue and mauve. Also slightly lime-tolerant.
'**The Great Mogul**' AGM 1.1m (44in), black-purple self.

Double (6-fall), or peony-flowered:
'**Beni-tsubaki**' 69cm (27in), rose violet, white veins and style arms.
'**Caprician Butterfly**' AGM 91cm (36in), purple standards edged white, falls white veined with purple, gold signals. Payne Medal (AIS).
'**Continuing Pleasure**' AGM 97cm (38in), deep violet-purple. May rebloom.
'**Flashing Koi**' 91cm (36in), white, with red-purple halo, veins and style arms.
'**Hercule**' 91cm (36in), large mid- to dark blue, deeper blue veins.
'**Katy Mendez**' AGM 70cm (28in) mid-violet with darker veins, yellow signals.
'**Kuma-funjin**' 91cm (36in), very deep purple-blue.
'**Light at Dawn**' 81cm (32in), white with narrow blue borders.
'**Moonlight Waves**' 91cm (36in), white with greenish hafts, semi-double.
'**Oriental Eyes**' 91cm (36in), light violet shading to grey-white, purple halo and veins. Payne Medal.
'**Pink Frost**' 1.02m (41in), light orchid-pink self.
'**Summer Storm**' AGM 1.07m (42in), dark purple with extra styles and petaloids. May rebloom.

Eye Shadow Irises which are hybrids between *I. pseudacorus* and *I. ensata* are being bred in Japan, following on from earlier work on such hybrids. Vigorous plants with green leaves, the flowers shown in photographs are white, yellow, bronze, pink, violet or near-orange, or combine two or more colours, with sharply outlined signals. Some have toning or contrasting veins. It is to be hoped that they will reach other countries before long.

LOUISIANA IRISES

In spite of their name, these irises (Series Hexagonae) are native to several southern states of the USA, from Florida to Texas, with two hardier species, coppery-orange *Iris fulva* and the lovely blue *I. brevicaulis*, found as far north as Missouri and some Midwest states. These two, and the hybrid between them, *I.* x *fulvala* AGM with glowing purple flowers, will flower outside in warmer parts of Britain. The problem with other species and many cultivars bred in the USA and Australia is that they will usually grow but do not flower well, if at all, in cooler climates.

Iris fulva, 50-91cm (20-36in), can vary slightly in colour and has a yellow form. Much shorter, 15-30cm (6-12in), *I. brevicaulis* has a zigzag stem. Although both need a moist soil, it should not be waterlogged, but *I.* x *fulvala* needs damper conditions, even a bog. All need plenty of sun in Britain and to have the rhizomes at or just below the soil surface; if their evergreen leaves are damaged in winter the plants suffer a setback. They can be grown in pots in a cold greenhouse, as can modern cultivars, with the pots (except for those holding the two species above) standing in water. One older cultivar which flowers fairly well in a warm British garden, planted by a shallow pool which overflows, is the bright blue **'Clyde Redmond'**.

A wide range of cultivars is available in the USA and Louisiana Irises are proving very successful in parts of Australia, especially New South Wales, where several have won Dykes Medals.

OTHER BEARDLESS SPECIES

The hardiest iris of all is *Iris setosa* AGM, since it grows as far north as the Arctic Circle in Siberia. It is also found in northern China and Japan and across the Bering Strait in North America, mainly Alaska and Labrador but further south too. As a result it does not cope well with hotter climates nor with dry conditions but is still an excellent iris for the majority of temperate gardens with neutral to mildly acid, moisture-retentive but not boggy soil. Plant 2-5cm (1-2in) deep in sun or part shade. Colours include blue- and red-purple, lavender-pink, and white, with intermediate shades. The falls are quite large, perhaps compensating for the tiny standards, which are often reduced to bristles. Stem heights range from 30 to 91cm (1-3ft), taller forms having good branching and numerous flowers. *I.s.* subsp. *hondoensis*, with deep purple, velvety flowers, is one such. Slightly shorter, good whites are *I.s.* **'Alba'** and *I.s.* **'Kosho-en'**, the latter with dark spathes setting off the flowers. There is a form, rare as yet, with variegated leaves.

Iris hookeri, still often found as *I. setosa* var. *canadensis* or *I.s.* 'Nana', is only 15-22cm (6-9in) tall, with slatey-blue flowers that may have enlarged, almost horizontal, standards; it likes a moist spot in the rock garden. *I. setosa* var. *arctica,* another dwarf, is also found under the names above, but has purple flowers with white markings.

The other member of Series *Tripetalae*, *Iris tridentata* from the southeastern USA, needs summer warmth though it survives New England winters where it flowers late, in July, and is stoloniferous. It is not reliably hardy in Britain but can be grown under glass. Its flowers are similar to those of *I. setosa.*

Like those above, another North American native, *Iris prismatica*, is deciduous, but this is hardy. The flowers have narrow but pretty petals in blue-violet, white, pink or with plicata markings. It is stoloniferous and prefers acid, fairly moist but not soggy soil; heavy clay, especially in wet winters, does not suit it. Fine grassy leaves surround the 30-80cm (12-32in) stems.

A well known, good garden iris, valued for its evergreen foliage and especially for its seeds in winter, as they do not drop from the pods but stay in place till spring, is *Iris foetidissima* AGM. Native to Europe, including Britain, and North Africa, it will grow almost anywhere, even in dry shade under trees, but responds to better treatment. It is tolerant of most soils, prefers some moisture (but is not a water iris) and some sunshine. The shining green leaves catch the light, particularly in winter when they set off the pods of red, orange, or yellow seeds. *I.f.* **'Fructu Albo'** is the white-seeded form. The flowers, usually a mixture of mauve and brown, are subdued but there are more noticeable bluer forms as well as the yellows of *I.f.* var. *citrina*, *I.f.* var. *lutescens* and *I.f.* **'Moonshy'**. Between four and seven are borne on short branches, on 35-46cm (14-18in) stems, in midsummer. It has the British names of gladdon, gladwyn, or stinking iris, the latter because the leaves smell unpleasant, briefly, if they are cut or bruised. In *I.f.* **'Variegata'** AGM they are striped with white, decorating the garden all year round, but the plant is less ready to flower and set seed and less vigorous. Like other beardless irises, it is easier to establish as a small clump than single rhizomes.

More American natives include *Iris missouriensis* AGM from the Rocky Mountains; this likes a limy soil, not too dry, and full sun. The name *I. longipetala* is now considered a synonym as *I. missouriensis* can be quite variable as to flower colour, basically white with many blue-purple to lilac veins. The branched stems are 20-91cm (8-36in) tall and it is semi-evergreen, so is best divided and replanted as soon as flowering ends, in June in Britain. *I.* 'Tol-long' AGM has pale violet, veined flowers. *Iris verna* is less easy to keep in cultivation, though as it is quite widespread in some eastern and central US states it seems easier there; it likes some shade and well-drained acid soil. The light violet-blue flowers, with orange-lined white signals on the falls, are relatively large for its tiny stems.

Iris lactea AGM (syn. *I. biglumis*) is an easy iris for well-drained limy soil. When established it will stand drought but the roots should not be allowed to dry out when it is transplanted. Widespread throughout much of Asia, including Korea and China, the deciduous leaves are used for fodder and for making ropes and string. The fragrant blue-violet to white flowers are carried on unbranched 5-30cm (2-12in) stems. At one time it had the name *I. ensata* and there are man-made hybrids with Sino-Siberian cultivars called Chrysatas, which should be grown like the Sino-Siberians.

A dwarf species, *Iris ruthenica,* has stems up to 20cm (8in) with dark violet flowers, the falls veined or dotted on a white ground. *I.r.* var. *nana* is very tiny, stems from 2cm (1in) tall, and can be lighter in colour, and *I.r.* var. *brevituba* f. *leucantha* is white. All are fairly easy in the rock garden, in a light but moderately rich, lime-free soil in sun or part shade, or the alpine house. That is the safest place, as a rule, for two species in Subgenus *Nepalensis*, though they can be tried outside in sunny places if they are kept consistently moist from mid-spring to mid-autumn but are kept dry, or lifted and stored in dry sand or peat, once the leaves die back. Both have tiny rhizomes or growing points with fleshy roots that need careful handling. *Iris decora* is 10-30cm (4-12in) tall, *I. collettii* up to 5cm (2in), and their pale purple flowers are pretty but very short-lived.

There are many more species than can be mentioned here, some presenting a challenge to the grower but very rewarding when they succeed, as they may do if the right conditions can be provided. The book *A Guide to Species Irises* has a wealth of information, including cultural advice.

Iris foetidissima AGM

Bulbous Irises

THESE STORE FOOD IN BULBS instead of rhizomes and there are several different groups. The little Reticulata Irises belong to Subgenus *Hermodactyloides* and are the earliest to bloom, starting in late winter when, or where, the weather is mild. Also well known, but flowering in late spring to midsummer, is Subgenus *Xiphium*, the Dutch hybrids so often seen in florists' shops, the less sturdy Spanish irises and, later, the so-called 'English' irises, *Iris latifolia*. Flowering in the intervening period, with some overlap at either end, are the Juno Irises, Subgenus *Scorpiris*.

They are plants for sunny spots in the garden, many but not all needing a thorough baking after they have flowered, to build up reserves for the next year's performance. They can be helped by feeding with bonemeal, or a high-potash fertiliser, after flowering finishes, and this also assists the offsets around the parent bulb to grow on. Not all, however, are hardy enough for the open garden - this is especially true of many Junos - or it may not be possible for them to be kept dry enough; also small bulbs can be overgrown by other plants. For all these reasons, cultivation in pots or a bulb frame can be more satisfactory, and some that cannot be safely grown outside in Britain are mentioned in the chapter on Growing Under Glass.

RETICULATA IRISES
January, in Britain, may see **Iris histrioides** and its named forms producing their sizeable violet-blue flowers, the style arms and crests very prominent and the falls marked in white, yellow and dark violet. A little later, **Iris reticulata** AGM begins. This dark violet, smaller-flowered species gives the group its name and is a parent of numerous hybrids, such as wine-purple **I.r. 'J.S. Dijt'**. Other hybrids, with intermediate-sized flowers and heights around 10-15 cm (4-6in), have been bred from crosses between *I. reticulata* and *I. histrioides*, or *I. reticulata* and the closely related, pale blue and purple, *I. bakeriana*.

Smaller **Iris danfordiae** is only 5-7cm (2-in) tall but its bright lemon-yellow colour is cheerful. Its standards are only tiny bristles but other parts a good size. Getting the bulbs to flower in later years is not easy as they split into many 'rice-grain' bulblets which may eventually reach flowering size if the original bulbs are planted in light soil, 25cm (10in) deep, and fed heavily with bonemeal for at least three years. Or one can benefit from the expertise of professional growers and buy new bulbs each year; they are relatively cheap.

Paler yellow flowers, the same size as those of *Iris histrioides,* are borne by *I. winogradowii* AGM, which needs more moisture than other reticulatas. The bulbs should not dry out completely. These two species have been hybridised to produce several excellent cultivars 7cm (3in) tall, strong growers for sunny positions in the rock garden or troughs, bulb frame or pots. **'Katharine Hodgkin'** AGM has pale yellow flowers marked with blue, **'Frank Elder'** is bluer and **'Sheila Ann Germaney'**, still rare, more purple-blue.

Virtually all the Reticulata group can be recommended, including those named above. **'George'** AGM is an outstanding, robust and reliable hybrid between 'J.S. Dijt' and *I. histrioides*. A very new introduction, **'Agatha Dawson'**, has leaves lined with creamy yellow and dark purple flowers.

JUNO IRISES

There are many species of Juno irises, probably more than in any other subgenus, but very few can be grown in the garden and they must have very sunny places, possibly sheltered too, and first-class drainage. The rock garden or the top of a dry wall may be suitable. If in doubt grow them under glass where others that are less difficult can be tried, but many are rare and need extremely careful treatment.

Junos store food in their bulbs and also in thick fleshy roots that grow beneath them. These are essential for them to survive and if lost or damaged the bulb will almost certainly die. Buying them in pots, as growing plants, ensures a good start but if they are bare-rooted or when it is time to re-pot, handle them gently. A series of leaves grows up the stem, making some resemble small maize plants, and there are buds growing from some axils (leaf joints) as well as at the terminal. Most flowers are quite large and showy, certainly as regards the style arms and crests, and the standards are usually small and turned right down. A central ridge or crest decorates the falls. Hardy and easy to grow in most places with the right conditions, *Iris bucharica* AGM has glossy green leaves on stems up to 40cm (16in), with up to six white flowers with yellow falls. There is an all-yellow form that may be incorrectly labelled *I. orchioides* but that species is less hardy. *I. cycloglossa* is a very attractive plant, 20-40cm (8-16in) tall, with quite large lavender flowers with semi-erect standards. Other possibles, similar in height, for out of doors include *I. graeberiana*, lavender with white on the falls and a white ridge, or yellow falls; *I. magnifica* AGM, pale lilac, or white in *I.m.* **'Alba'**. Shelter is really needed by *I. aucheri*, which can be pale blue or any shade between white and deep violet, up to 35cm (14in) tall, and *I. warleyensis*, which is violet with yellow crests and 20-40cm (8-16in) in height.

Iris aucheri was formerly called *I. sindjarensis* and was crossed with the more tender *I. persica* to give the hybrid **'Sindpers'** AGM, which is reasonably hardy, 25cm (10in) tall, with greenish-blue flowers. A cross with *I. warleyensis* produced **'Warlsind'**, yellow and blue, 25-35cm (10-14in) tall, and also fairly hardy.

SUBGENUS *XIPHIUM*

For much of the year, thanks to special treatments, it is possible to buy irises of this subgenus from florists. Most often they are the 'Dutch' hybrids though others may appear occasionally. The range of colours offered does tend to be rather limited and buying from bulb catalogues gives a wider choice for cutting or as attractive companions for other plants. They are easy to grow and given the right conditions will increase steadily each year. Being planted 5cm (2in) deep in sunny, well-drained places with a little fertiliser (not manure) forked in after flowering suits the majority; *Iris latifolia* needs more moisture.

Iris xiphium is known as the Spanish Iris though it grows in other countries around the Mediterranean, and is the earliest to flower, starting in late spring. Shorter, at 40-61cm (16-24in), and more slender than other xiphiums, the flowers are blue, violet or white. *I.x.* var. *lusitanica* is yellow, *I.x.* var. *battandieri* white with orange on its falls, and the large blue flowers of *I.x.* var. *praecox* appear earlier than the rest. Sometimes named cultivars can be obtained: **'Cajanus'** is yellow, **'King of the Blues'** deep blue, and **'Thunderbolt'** has purple-brown standards and brown falls with a yellow blotch. But an unnamed mixture is more frequently offered.

Other species are less hardy and in Britain are best under glass, though with shelter *Iris tingitana* may be possible. Up to three blue flowers are borne on 61cm (24in) tall stems, and from this species crossed with *I. xiphium* have come the cultivars mainly developed in Holland. Colours include blue, violet, purple, white, yellow, orange and bronze, separately or combined. They too may be offered as mixtures. It is best to buy the largest bulbs available, though some such as **'Yellow Queen'** do not make large bulbs. Smaller bulbs giving only one flower are generally used by commercial cut flower producers but larger bulbs should produce two.

'Professor Blaauw' AGM is an excellent dark violet-blue garden variety and is good for cutting too. Other reliable cultivars include:

'Amber Beauty' yellow bitone, tall, vigorous.

'Apollo' in palest blue and bright yellow.

'Blue Elegance' purple standards and blue falls.

'Bronze Queen' yellowish brown.

'Cream Beauty' white, cream and yellow.

'Duchy Blue' violet-blue bitone.;
'Gipsy Beauty' with blue standards and bronze falls.
'Lemon Queen'
'Mauve King'
'Oriental Beauty' blue standards and yellow falls.
'White Excelsior'

A species that will die if kept too dry in summer is the so-called 'English' iris, *I. latifolia* AGM (syn. *I. xiphioides*, sometimes *I. anglica)*, actually native to northwest Spain and the Pyrenees but at one time widely grown in western England. Taller and sturdier than the Mediterranean species, around 75cm (30in), its flowers are most commonly dark violet-blue but there are red-purple, pale blue, lilac-pink and white variants. In the late 19th century all these and others, including striped flowers, were offered but lost favour (and perhaps vigour) and only the very good white *I.l.* **'Mont Blanc'** seemed to have survived. Recently some named cultivars have come back into commerce: blue *I.l.* **'Duchess of York'**, lilac-rose *I.l.* **'Isabella'**, *I.l.* **'King of the Blues'** in rich dark blue, wine-purple *I.l.* **'Mansfield'** and pale *I.l.* **'Queen of the Blues'** along with *I.l.* **'Mont Blanc'**. The bulbs are quite large, covered with a hairy tunic, and should be planted about 7cm (3in) deep in moisture-retentive but not soggy soil in sun. Darker flecking on the flowers may be due to virus but it does not seem to affect the vigour of the plants or be transmitted to other irises.

Growing Irises under Glass

ONE GOOD REASON FOR GROWING some irises under glass is that though they may be able to tolerate cold, even a little frost, it is too much wet, especially in winter, that is likely to be fatal. A cold greenhouse, bulb frame or alpine house extends the range that can be successfully grown with the right cultivation, but it may not be possible to have all the irises that are mentioned below in the same environment.

Ventilation is extremely important, since it is not necessarily enough to provide a free-draining compost, such as JI No 3 in Britain, mixed with an equal quantity of grit, plus magnesian limestone for irises that need it, topped with grit around the rhizomes or the necks of bulbs. Atmospheric moisture, especially if there is no air movement, can lead to rot, as can careless watering. Always water from below, only when it is really needed in winter and rarely if at all in summer, though when growth is active in spring and autumn plants will need more. If water must be given from above, do not let it get into the foliage.

Irises that need to be kept completely dry from the time flowering ends until autumn, then be watered sparingly until spring, can be grown in pots unless, like most arilbreds, they are too vigorous and need space in a bulb frame. Walls of concrete blocks, two or three blocks high, with a cold frame on top, are easy to construct and should be filled with the same compost mixture as above but with a low-nitrogen fertiliser added. A higher frame can have the bottom 15cm (6in) or so filled with rubble for better drainage.

One group that does need more moisture is the cane-type Evansias. As well as those previously described that can be tried outside but may be safer in large pots or beds in a cold greenhouse - that is, *Iris confusa, I. japonica* and its cultivars such as **'Bourne Graceful'** - there are *I. wattii*, which has large near-blue flowers, grows up to 2m (6ft+) and may need staking, and **'Bourne Noble'**, pale mauve and slightly shorter. The latter is an *I. wattii* hybrid and neither it nor its parent is hardy in Britain. Nor is *I. formosana*, which has big lilac-blue flowers. All need to be well fed and can make big plants.

In contrast, the *Oncocyclus* irises, many with very dramatically beautiful flowers, must have a dry atmosphere especially in summer, and an alkaline and very gritty compost, preferably in their own frame or bed in the alpine house. *Iris gatesii* has large blooms on 40cm (16in) tall stems, white, cream or pinkish with brown or deep purple speckles and dark signals. Heavy veining, particularly on the falls, decorates the white *I. iberica* and its subspecies, 20-30cm (8-12in) tall, and *I. sari*, which is yellowish with reddish to black veins, 6-30cm (2½ -12in). *I. barnumae* has several subspecies and forms, *I.b.* f. *barnumae* yellow, others purple, 10-25cm (4-10in) tall. *The Guide to Species Irises* gives more detailed advice as well as information on other species.

Somewhat easier to accommodate are the Regelias, Pseudoregelias, and Regelio-cyclus hybrids that can be tried out of doors if conditions are right. Under glass they need room to spread, such as a frame. *Iris hoogiana* and *I. stolonifera* have been described earlier, and another *Regelia* is *I. korolkowii*, 20-30cm (8-12in) tall with heavily veined pale flowers. Lilac *I. cuniculiformis*, *I. narcissiflora*, yellow, and *I. kemaonensis*, which has lilac-purple flowers with deeper blotches on tiny stems, are Pseudoregelias which may be suitable for pots, and others in this Section are worth seeking out.

Iris decora and *I. collettii* were mentioned earlier as being safer in the alpine house unless conditions outside are right. *I. speculatrix* from Hong Kong, with lavender flowers on 20-30cm (8-12in) stems, needs plenty of light and can barely tolerate frost. The hardy Reticulatas can be grown in deep pots (and can be brought indoors when in bloom) or a bulb frame, protecting the flowers from weather and slugs. Smaller species, blue *I. hyrcana*, blue and purple *I. pamphylica*, and *I. kolpakowskiana*, lilac-violet, all less than 10cm (4in) tall, are safer in pots or a frame. *I. filifolia*, 25-45cm (10-18in) with reddish-purple and orange flowers is a tender Xiphium for a frame and so is yellow *I. juncea*.

Juno irises need 'long tom' pots or a frame. The hardier ones can be grown this way if not outside. Many are not hardy, or need protection from too much wet at the wrong time. *I. orchioides* is yellow, 30cm (12in) tall; *I. vicaria* violet and yellow, 35cm (14in); *I. kopetdaghensis* greenish yellow, 25cm (10in) or more tall. Shorter ones include *I. willmottiana* in lavender with blue flecking, and *I.w.* **'Alba'**, 15cm (6in), and the variable 10cm (4in) tall *I. nicolai* in several colour forms.

Further Reading

Austin, C. *Iris, the classic bearded varieties* Quadrille Publishing Ltd., 2001

Cassidy, G.E. & Linnegar, S. *Growing Irises* Christopher Helm, 1988 *O/P*

Cayeux, R. *L'Iris, Une Fleur Royale* Mauryflor, France, 1996. (In French)

Dykes, W.R. *The Genus Iris* 1913. Facsimile edition, Dover Books, 1975

Glasgow, K. *Irises, A Practical Gardening Guide* Godwit Publishing Ltd., NZ, 1996, Batsford, UK, 1997

Grosvenor, G. *Iris, Flower of the Rainbow* Kangaroo Press Pty. Ltd., Australia, 1997

Kohlein, Fritz *Iris* Ulmer 1981 (in German), Christopher Helm, 1988 (translated by Timber Press, 1987). *O/P*

Linnegar, S. & Hewitt, J. *Irises* RHS Wisley Handbook, 2003

Mathew, B. *The Iris* 2nd edition. Batsford, 1989 *O/P*

McEwen, Currier *The Siberian Iris* Timber Press, 1992

- *The Japanese Iris* University Press of New England, 1990

Shear, Wm. *The Gardener's Iris Book* The Taunton Press, USA, 1998

Stebbings, G. *The Gardener's Guide to Growing Irises* David & Charles, Timber Press, 2001

The Society for Louisiana Irises, *The Louisiana Iris* Timber Press, 2nd edition 2000

The Species Group of the British Iris Society, *A Guide to Species Irises* Cambridge University Press, 1997.

Waddick, James & Yu-tang, Zhao *Iris of China* Timber Press, 1992

O/P indicates that these titles were out of print at the time this booklet was published; it may be possible to obtain second-hand copies of these books.

Where to see and buy Irises

Many gardens open to the public have irises, often in mixed plantings. The following are some where irises may be seen in quantity.

RHS Gardens, Wisley, Woking, Surrey GU23 6QB. The Trials Field has the main cultivar groups and many irises are planted elsewhere.

Royal Botanic Gardens, Kew, Richmond, Surrey TW9 3AB. Species irises of many types.

Royal Botanic Gardens Kew, Wakehurst Place, Ardingly, West Sussex RH17 6TN. Japanese (*Iris ensata*) cultivars and other irises.

BIS Garden at The Gardens of the Rose, Royal National Rose Society, Chiswell Green, St Albans, Herts. AL2 3NR. Bearded and beardless cultivars. Opening times are limited so check first. ☎ 01727 850461.

Lingen Nursery and Garden, Lingen, Bucknell, Shropshire SY7 0DY. NCCPG National Collection of *Iris sibirica* cultivars.

Marwood Hill Gardens, Marwood, Barnstaple, Devon EX31 4EB. NCCPG National Collection of *Iris ensata* cultivars.

Rowden Gardens, Brentor, Tavistock, Devon PL19 0NG. NCCPG National Collection of Water Irises.

The University of Birmingham Botanic Garden, 58 Edgbaston Park Road, Edgbaston Birmingham, B15 2RT. NCCPG National collection of *Iris unguicularis* and *I. lazica*.

Myddelton House Gardens, Bulls Cross, Enfield, EN2 9HG. NCCPG National Collection of award-winning bearded irises.

NURSERIES:
United Kingdom

Irises are available from many nurseries listed in *The RHS Plant Finder,* which is published annually. Specialist nurseries and general ones with good numbers of irises are listed below.

Aulden Farm, Aulden, Leominster, Herefordshire HR6 0JT. ☎ 01568 720219. Website: www.auldenfarm.co.uk Japanese Iris cvs. and other beardless irises.

Claire Austin Hardy Plants, The Stone House, Cramp Pool, Shifnal, Shropshire TF11 8PE. ☎ 01952 463700. Website: www.claireaustin-hardyplants.co.uk Wide range.

Avon Bulbs, Burnt House Farm, Mid Lambrook, South Petherton, Somerset TA13 5HE. ☎ 01460 242177. Website: www.avonbulbs.co.uk Bulbs, PCIs, Siberians.

Beeches Nursery, Ashdon, Saffron Walden, Essex CB10 2HB.
☎ 01799 584362. Website: www.beechesnursery.co.uk Wide range.
Broadleigh Gardens, Bishops Hull, Taunton, Somerset TA4 1AE.
☎ 01823 286231. Website: www.broadleighbulbs.co.uk Bulbs, PCIs, dwarf beardeds, species.
Cambridge Bulbs, 40 Whittlesford Road, Newton, Cambridge CB2 5PH.
☎ 01223 871760. Arils, arilbreds, bulbs, species.
Cotswold Garden Flowers, Sands Lane, Badsey, Evesham, Worcs. WR11 5EZ. ☎ 01386 422829. Website: www.cgf.net Bearded and beardless cvs.
Croftway Nursery, Yapton Road, Barnham, Bognor Regis, West Sussex P022 0BQ. ☎ 01243 552121. Website: www.croftway.co.uk Beardeds, Siberians.
Barry Emmerson, 24 Seaward Avenue, Leiston, Suffolk IP16 4BB.
☎ 01728 832650. Tall bearded cvs.
Famecheck Special Plants, Hilltrees, Wandlebury Hill, Cambridge CB2 4AD. ☎ 01223 243734. Bearded cvs.
The Iris Garden, 47 Station Road, Barnet, Herts. EN5 1PR. ☎ 0208 441 1300. Website: www.theirisgarden.co.uk Tall and other bearded and spuria cvs.
Kelways, Barrymore Farm, Langport, Somerset TA10 9EZ.
☎ 01458 250521. Website: www.kelways.co.uk Wide range.
Lingen Nursery and Garden, Lingen, Bucknell, Shropshire SY7 0DY ☎ 01544 267720. Website: www.lingennursery.co.uk Siberian cvs, species, shorter beardeds.
Potterton & Martin, The Cottage Nursery, Moortown Road, Nettleton, Caistor, Lincs. LN7 6HX. ☎ 01472 851714.
Website: www.users.globalnet.co.uk/~pottin Arils, bulbs, species.
Rowden Gardens, Brentor, Tavistock, Devon PL19 0NG.
☎ 01822 810275. Japanese and Siberian cvs, water irises especially *Iris versicolor* cvs.
Seagate Irises, Long Sutton By-pass, Long Sutton, Lincs PE12 9RX.
☎ 01406 365138. Website: www.irises.co.uk Bearded cvs.
Westonbirt Plants, 9 Westonbirt Close, Worcester WR5 3RX.
☎ 01905 350429. Bulbs, especially Junos, PCIs, species.
Zephyrwude Irises, 48 Blacker Lane, Crigglestone, Wakefield, West Yorkshire WF4 3EW. ☎ 01924 252101. Bearded cvs, especially shorter ones.

Europe

Cayeux S.A., Boite Postale 35, 45501 GIEN Cedex, France ☎ 0800 096 4811. Website; www.cayeux.fr Bearded cvs. Catalogue in English.

Dr T. Tamberg, Zimmerstr. 3, 12207 Berlin, Germany
☎ (0049)(0)30 712 4235.
Website: www.http.//home.t-online.de/home/Dr.T.u.C.Tamberg/
Siberians, unusual beardless hybrids. Catalogue in English.

USA

Cooley's Iris Gardens, P.O. Box 126, Silverton, OR 97381-0126. Bearded cvs.
Schreiner's Iris Gardens, 3629 Quinaby Road, Salem, Oregon 97303.
Wide range.
Many other iris nurseries advertise in the AIS *Bulletin*, which can be
borrowed from the BIS Library by members, and is sent to AIS members.

Australia

Rainbow Ridge Nursery, Taylor Road, Dural, New South Wales 2158.
Bearded and Louisiana cvs.
Tempo Two, P.O. Box 60A, Pearcedale, Victoria 3912. Wide range.

New Zealand

Mossburn Iris Gardens, P.O. Box 96, Mossburn. Wide range.
Maritima, 2 Worcester Street, Hampden, North Otago. Species and other
irises.
Richmond Iris Garden, 376 Hill Street, Richmond, Nelson. Bearded cvs.

SPECIALIST SOCIETIES

The British Iris Society, Hon. Secretary, 40 Willow Park, Otford,
Sevenoaks, Kent TN14 5NF. ☎ 01959 523017. Email:
hilarytowers@aol.com. Website: www.britishirissociety.org.uk Publishes
The Iris Year Book (annually), booklets on cultivation and other iris matters,
newsletters, seed list. Regional and specialist groups. Shows and meetings.
Extensive library and slide library for members' use.
The American Iris Society, Sara R. Marley, Secretary, 843 Co. Rd. 3,
Hannibal, NY 13074, USA. Website: www.irises.org Publishes *The
Bulletin* (four times a year). Regional societies. Specialist Sections.
Iris Society of Australia, c/o Mr J. Roberts, PO Box 457, Emerald,
Victoria 3782, Australia.
New Zealand Iris Society, c/o Mr H. Collins, 6 Pye's Pa Road,
Tauranga, New Zealand.
There are iris societies in many other countries. If help is needed, the BIS
Hon. Membership Secretary, 15 Parkwood Drive, Rawtenstall, Lancs. BB4
6RP, may be able to supply addresses.

Other Booklets in the HPS Series

- CAMPANULAS IN THE GARDEN

- EPIMEDIUMS AND OTHER HERBACEOUS BERBERIDACEAE

- EUPHORBIAS

- GRASSES

- HARDY GERANIUMS FOR THE GARDEN

- HOSTAS

- PENSTEMONS

- PHLOX

- PULMONARIAS

- SAXIFRAGACEAE - *Some herbaceous members of the Saxifragaceae family*

- UMBELLIFERS

- SUCCESS WITH SEEDS

Apart from *Success with Seeds*, which is a practical guide to collecting, germinating seed and growing on the resultant plants, each booklet provides comprehensive and practical information on garden-worthy plants in its genus. As well as an invaluable A to Z of species and cultivars, the booklets deal with topics such as cultivation, pests and diseases, propagation, and plant associations. Most booklets include appendices giving information on where to see and where to buy the listed plants. The series has been well received and booklets have attracted excellent reviews.